# A Whiter Shade of Trash

by

# Fats Beauregard

*To Carolyn, for keeping Friday Night alive and, more importantly, for being you. . .*

Disclaimer

Except perhaps for myself, probably no one in the book is blameless. Everyone has flaws. But none of the people whose story I try to relate in this book are representative of the fine people of the South who are generally upright, friendly and generous.--FB

Most of the events in this book—from Chapter 2 to the Conclusion—took place between Dec 2013 and Sept 2015.

# Table of Contents

A
Whiter
Shade
of
Trash

# Chapter 1 Worse than "Honey Boo Boo"

This book is mainly about some people I've met since I moved to Mississippi in 2011 and our activities together as we tried to create a hit Reality TV Show on a very small budget. Those who remember Howard Stern's low budget Channel Nine (WWOR) show in the early 90's might appreciate that quality television can be made on a very low budget, not that our show was ever as funny. If our show was funny, it was more in the funny peculiar rather than funny ha ha sense. Our budget, though, for the pilot and first season was less than half of the Stern Show budget for a single episode. But first let me tell you how this all started.

For around two years I was living in a trailer with this guy Glen who I met in an internet chat room. Wait wait wait wait wait! We were NOT gay or anything like that. I am not gay! He lived on one end of this 80 foot motor home with his Chihuahuas and a cat and I lived in the other end with my internet porn and a really large bathroom. Sometimes we'd sit in the living room and talk or watch TV, but that was about it. Didn't want you to think anything weird was going on.

Anyway, after nearly two years, he's driving home from work and picks up a woman hitchhiking, wearing "the shortest dress I've seen in years" and hooks up with her and disappears for over half a week. As it turned out, they both worked at the same Walmart, though usually on different shifts. Before he met her, I don't think he'd gotten laid in four or five years. He also claimed that he didn't masturbate which could either mean that he was horny as hell or horny as hell and a compulsive liar too. I figure the latter more likely because I believe anyone who says they don't masturbate was a compulsive liar. (I believe the same about people who say they never lie also being compulsive liars, but then again, I never lie so I could be wrong about that.) Being an extremely humble person, I try to give people the benefit of the doubt and I try to not judge people.

After four days of him not being around, there's a lot of dog shit all over the living room—mainly on the floor. We also started running low of dog and cat food. I didn't mind feeding his pets when he wasn't there, but I wasn't going to clean up after them. Anyway, I text-ed him to let him know about the dog and cat food situation and that it was his day off and reminded him that he needed to get some sleep. He always slept 20 to 24 or more hours straight on his first day off, but I guess he liked having sex with his new girlfriend more than he liked sleeping. This one fact indicated that he was in some serious shit—perhaps even what they sometimes call "in love."

The following day, a Friday—the fifth day of his new romance—he showed up with Dog and Cat Food. One of the first things he said was: "Man, after you text-ed me about sleeping, she asked me if we were gay. You really got me into some trouble."

"Sorry, but I was concerned. . . I thought you would be really stressed out about missing your usual 24 hours of sleep from when you got off work Thursday morning." At that time, he worked the Graveyard shift for around a year, getting Thursdays/Fridays and Fridays/Saturdays off and going back to work Saturday night at eleven. He worked at a Walmart around 40 miles from where he lived. His girlfriend worked the day shift. What he told me next lingered in my mind since he told it to me.

"This girls' family is crazy. They're worse than Honey Boo Boo." He then went on to describe how nasty and out of control the kids were. Apparently there were four kids ranging in age from 10 to 16 from "all different fathers"—actually, a girl and a boy were twins so I assumed they had the same father.

She had two other children—both boys—who weren't living with her.  All I know about them is the youngest was living with his father and the oldest had either run away from home, been kicked out of the house, was in a detention center, jail or prison or was, perhaps, a fugitive—or dead. . .

Anyway, they ended up getting engaged and got married a few months later.  I made a toast at the reception—using sparking grape juice since most of them were supposed to be in recovery for alcoholism or drug addiction—about how cynical I had become about concepts like true love, and how Glen (and Anne) proved me wrong and how he actually loved Anne more than he loved sleeping all day on his day off.

The following September his whole family, including the Anne's mother and grandmother, moved into a rent-to-own house in Bay St. Louis.  That was the last time I saw him, though he occasionally text-ed me, usually about sports—mainly the Dallas Cowboys and LSU football—and his pet chihuahua.

# Chapter 2 The Big Move

Three or four months later, Glen called me to see if I would print up some fliers with pictures of a couple chihuahua puppies he was trying to sell. Since my printer was out of ink and I didn't know if it would work with my new computer, I had to turn him down. We talked for five or ten minutes and then, in the background, Anne said something to him and he said:

"Anne reminded me to tell you that her mother is thinking of moving out. She was wondering if you'd be interested in moving down here and renting a room from us. You must be really lonely up there in Picayune and we would give you a really good price."

"I don't know," I said. "I have the princess [the bastard left me with his cat when he moved] to keep me company. And I don't know if I could afford electricity and internet down there in addition to the rent. The electric bill in the summer must be a killer."

"You'd pay the same amount every month with utilities included. We'd agree on a price before we did this and it would be less than what you pay for everything up there. And it's a nice neighborhood within walking distance to the gulf. And you'd have full access to the kitchen, washer, dryer, and cable TV. And there will always be someone around so you won't be lonely."

I don't know why he thought I was so lonely. Actually, what I was thinking about was when he said Anne's family was worse than Honey Boo Boo's which got my mental gears going about developing a reality TV show about his family. This is something that I had been thinking about for years. Since the Osborne's anyway or maybe Big Brother, whichever was first.

"I still play the guitar," I said. "Maybe I'll make too much noise."

"The walls are pretty think and we could always turn the TV louder."

"I don't know.  Maybe if we could get Courtesy Flush reunited—not that we ever had a drummer of a decent vocalist. Would you be interested in getting the band going again?  I know Mark [our bassist] wants to."

"Of course I am.  Just have to get my guitar out of the pawn shop.  Two or three of Anne's kids can sing."

I was just about ready to ask if any of the kids could sing, so I was glad he said it instead.  I said:

"Then all we'd need is a drummer and we'd be set!"

This I decided to make pretend to be thinking about making a web cam program.  This was a real stretch, but I threw out this line of BS to him."

"But I might have to wait 5 or 6 months before I can move," I added.  "I forgot to tell you that I'm writing a book about when I hitched across the country when I was a kid and got picked up by nut who is believed to be the serial killer known as the I-10 Terminator.  While I'm writing it, I thought about turning it into an internet reality TV show so hopefully people who saw the show would buy the book."  I had thought about writing a book about this experience for years and even started it a couple times, but the memories we so bad that I didn't like to think about them.  Of course, the internet reality TV program was just a troll line I floated to get his reaction.

"You could probably do that here."

"Are you sure your family wouldn't freak out?  You don't live that far from I-10.  And the whole point of the show, which I would hope to get picked up by Court TV, or something like that, maybe even A&E or maybe the Learning or History Channel, would be how scared I am that he might decide to finish me off.  In each episode I would describe one of the murders he is believed to have committed.  This would, of course, be a big departure from the fiction I usually crap out."

I was realistic about my Antonina Lipski, aka Ann Lip, Bounty Hunter books to know that they were crap.  I will always deny that they are a rip off of Elaine Evanovich's Stephanie Plum novels citing the most obvious differences, Plum lived in Mercer County, NJ while Lipski lived in Morris County, NJ and while Plum was a slut who fucked cops, Lipski was a nymphomaniac who fucked criminals.  My books were not bestsellers but they sold enough to gain a faithful audience so that I always earned, on average, between $1000 and $5000 a month.  Sometimes more, almost never less, thought in July and August of 2008 I only earned $870 and $932.

"I doubt if they would be scared with you living in the same house.  Shit, if it's actually on TV, they'll probably all want to be on the show."  Hook, line, sinker—fish fry and gumbo!

It would, of course, be such a long shot finding a channel that would broadcast my silly premise about a writer writing about a serial killer that I never actually considered it and even a web cast made no sense.  Seriously, who wants to watch a writer write?  The idea though, was what I'd call a McGuffin, nothing but a plot element to get Glen's family interest about possibly having their own 15 minutes.  I didn't really want to write a book about the I-10 Terminator either and planned that after a few months writing, or pretending to write, I'd decide it was too hard and come up with another somewhat more novel idea.  A reality show about the Morgan family—a poor white religious family living in the mainly black part of town.  Even if they're not as out of control as Glen originally said they were, I was sure I could come up with a pilot that I might be able to sell to one of the five hundred or so cable networks looking for a gimmick to pull in some viewers.  Some might say that I would have to be an egomaniac to believe I could come up with a--hopefully hit—reality show with almost no budget or crew and I would have to agree with them.  Fortunately, I have enough humility to balance my ego with the belief that we shape our own reality.

We settled on a price of $500 a month for the room with cable and AC. This was expensive for Mississippi, but not for New Jersey, where I was originally from. I moved in around two weeks after Anne's Mother moved out.

Anne's grandmother lived in a small trailer on the side of the house but she used the bathroom that I shared with Anne's son Billy. The only other bathroom was between Anne and Glen's room and the room the three daughters shared. Of course, the one thing I hated more than fleas, was sharing a bathroom. It was why I moved out of New Jersey in the first place.

Bath or no bath, the wheels were spinning in my head. I've always been one to see potential and if nothing else, I was saving money just by moving. Who knows, maybe I could write a book about the serial killer. It couldn't be that much harder than writing fiction.

Or could it?

I called Arthur and he was willing to finance the cameras, web cams and sound equipment and whatever else I might need for the web cast and possible pilot. It was hard to imagine anyone who would want to watch a writer write. But they believed me. . .

# Chapter 3 *The Trap of the Terminator*

by Fats Beauregard

Dedicated to all the women I've had sex with, you know what you're missing!

When I was fourteen, in 1994, I ran away from the boarding school I was living at in Pennsylvania. My intention was to hitch to Seattle and form my own grunge band thinking that it would be taken more seriously if the group was from the birthplace of grunge, than the two bands I had already been in that we taken as jokes. I formed *Blind Boner* when I was in Middle School as well as my first incarnation of *Courtesy Flush*. Since it was late October and starting to get cold outside I decided to bum a ride to Florida from someone I knew who drove a truck there and back every week and then hitch west.

It was hard getting rides. I had a rather expensive guitar in a gig bag and most drivers probably thought I had a hatchet or an ax in it. It often took hours with my thumb out before getting a ride. It took four or five days to get across Texas when I got a ride to the middle of nowhere in Arizona.

It was there that I got into a car later believed to have been stolen and driven by the Serial Killer now known as I-10 Terminator. He laughed when I told him I had a Susanna Hoffs signature Rickenbacker guitar in my gig bag. He told me to hop in, and even offered me some Mad Dog wine which I gladly accepted. I should note here that even at the age of fourteen, I had what some would consider both alcohol and drug problems. The only problem I recognized at the time though, was getting it. I did have some success staying off hard drugs; sometimes anyway, but I loved whiskey, wine and weed. Beer too. And gin, vodka, rum and hash. And speed.

Instead of heading on to Los Angles, and then up to Seattle, I spent a few days paling around with Al—I refer to him as Al because he looked a little like the actor who played Al Bundy on *Married, With Children*, which was the best description I could give to the police. At some point he beat the crap out of me, tied me up in the cannon ball position, (as if I had jumped off a diving board doing a cannon ball) and buried me up to my neck in sand and put a metal bucket over my head.

I was lucky because two coeds in a dune buggy saw the bucket and one of them decided to use it for target practice. I made so much noise after a .22 pistol was fired that one of them lifted up the bucket and found me. Usually when I tell this story, which I've repeated a number of time, I usually lie and say the two beautiful coeds dug me out of the sand and then made mad passionate love to me, taking turns doing this, that and the other thing. But the truth is that they were scared to free me, probably thinking I'd want revenge for "nearly killing" me or because there was a "good reason" someone did that to me. Actually, I'm almost sure the one who fired missed the bucket, entirely. In any case, the one who fired the pistol drove off to get the authorities while the other stayed with me "to keep the vultures away." The police, along with some paramedics dug me out. Unfortunately, the I-10 Terminator took most of my clothes and all I was wearing was a pair of hi-cut shorts and, I guess, in Arizona this was a good enough reason to treat me like a male teen prostitute, rather than a crime victim. They didn't seem to care about me nearly being killed or that "Al" stole my 1988 Susanna Hoffs signature Rickenbacker guitar. I guess I should consider myself lucky that they didn't beat the crap out of me too. I was held in isolation—for my own good, they said—at a juvenile detention center until my father sent me enough money for cab fare to the

Phoenix airport, etc.

The cops must have taken me seriously enough to have filed a report because around five years later, shortly after I quit drinking, some FBI agents questioned me about what happened. They told me I was very lucky. I asked them when I could get it back. But instead of finding my Rickenbacker, they said I was lucky because I had almost certainly survived an encounter with the I-10 Terminator who had killed at least 15 people, probably a lot more. He would leave them, possibly still alive in some cases, often tied in the cannon ball position. There had been at least three or four previous victims before me and 12 or 13 more by 1998, when they questioned me. They found at least 20 more since then. I reiterated what I told the police in 1994, that he looked like the actor who played Al Bundy, but was probably only around 5'10" stating I could probably identify him in a lineup and could definitely identify my Jetglo Black Susanna Hoff signature Rickenbacker. They also asked me a few embarrassing questions, which I admitted might have been possible, but that I was too drunk to remember.

And that was it. Not much of a book. I could flesh things out. But not by much. I only remembered so much and there were somethings I didn't want to remember. I had seriously considered and have even started a few times writing a book about this. I also have to keep from incriminating myself in any of his crimes. Fortunately I knew him before he really got started on the murder side of things. I would have probably been only his third, forth or fifth victim, though we may never know how many were never found. I may have, in some way assisted him in seven armed robbery's (and there could have been some more we committed when I was so drunk that I just blacked out with no memory of). This was another reason why I wasn't more enthusiastic about the project. I doubt if I could use Stockholm syndrome as a defense, even though I was a somewhat unwilling accomplice. The fact that I was a juvenile and, hopefully, no one was hurt, might keep me from getting charged with anything. It was only after he started making sexual advances and telling me how pretty I was and how he'd only use the head, promising me it wouldn't hurt, etc, and finally asking me to kiss him that I decided to ask for a few dollars so I could catch a bus to LA, that he beat the crap out of me and brought me out into the desert to die.

Anyway, this was at least my third attempt at starting this book and it looked like the most I could get was three or four pages. I could write about each of his known victims, but that would take a lot of research. It does have a better title then my previous attempts at writing this: *Surviving Termination on I-10.* But I was already feeling like I've told more than I wanted to.

For the time being, I would only set up the web cams in my room and I wasn't in any great hurry to get online. If anyone actually wanted to watch me write, maybe I could set some sessions up. But it's a very boring process and watching it would only be more boring.

On the second day while I was writing, or pretending to be writing my masterpiece, granny—or Gram Gram as the kids usually call her—comes into my room and asked:

"Do you have any papers?"

Not getting it, I replied: "News Papers?"

"Rolling papers idiot!"

"Sorry no, I don't smoke."

She offered me enough Mississippi Mud Weed to make 5 blunts if I'd run up to the store to get some papers and "a bottle of Night Train" but I replied that I was really busy.

"How about if I take my teeth out and give you the best blow job you ever had?"

Now if I had already smoked some of that Mississippi Mud

Weed and drank a few bottles of Night Train, I might have taken her up on it, but I tried to turn her down as diplomatically as possible.

"Thanks for the offer. But I really am under a deadline here."

"You really a writer?"

"Most writers would probably consider me a hack because I believe word count is more important than literary pretensions." I heard or read that somewhere and it stuck with me. Still, I probably am more of a hack than most authors and I've never written anything that had really positive reviews.

I was hoping she'd go away, but she kept standing at my door. On the other hand, writing non-fiction is a lot harder than writing fiction and part of me enjoyed the distraction.

"Write any porn?"

"No," I said but then I thought about it. "I might spend enough time describing a sexual encounter to be considered pornographic in the same way Ulysses was considered pornography, but I would never get that deeply in details unless there was a reason for it so that the plot or something in the story line depended on it. And I never did it to titillate people. When I was younger I tried writing porn but it turned into political satire. I should have finished it and shopped it around. I predicted we'd have a Black Muslim vice president in the early 90s."

"Did he have a big dick? Most coloreds do you know."

"I never got around to measuring it. There were rumors that he was having inappropriate relations with a 13 years old girl, the daughter of the protagonist in the story, but I never really finished that part of the story—well, actually it was a play.

"Of course," I went on, "back then I did have literary pretensions. I even started it writing in blank verse. But I was still in my teens and many, if not most teenagers who write are, to some extant anyway, delusional."

"Tell me about the girl who fucked the nigga president?"

"In the first scene, someone, I forget who now, tried to bring it to the attention of her father who was the secretary of state or religion or something like that, that she had had sexual relations either with every boy in her class or possibly every boy in school.   Her name was Candy—Dupid I think.   Her father was Reverend Dupid.  Or something like that. I'm pretty sure it rhymed with 'stupid.'   At that time though, Malcolm Osmont was still the vice president.  He wasn't president until the first woman president got impeached when Candy's father had sex with her and realized that 'she' was actually a man in drag, which was the main plot hook of *The White Waterbed Incident.*  That and what happened when they tried to cover it up.  Although I find it hard to say anything good about Bill Clinton, he did inspire me to write this crap years before he 'invented oral sex with Monica' as Rush might say."

I couldn't believe I remembered all this crap.

I'll spare the reader what I don't want to spend any time talking about.  Let's just say she asked me to check a web link which had rather explicit pictures of her when she was 30, 40 or 50 years younger and I decided to get her the Night Train and rolling papers just to get rid of her.  There was also the possibility that if I kept talking to her, I'd get horny enough looking at the pictures to actually let her blow me.  She told me she'd pay me when I got back so I went to the convenience store and bought her some papers and a bottle of Night Train. As soon as I gave it to her, she asked me if I wanted to join her for a drink and smoke in her trailer—she wasn't allowed to drink or smoke weed in the house—and when I declined, she said she'd be right back with my money, but I guess she got busy drinking or smoking and forgot.  In any case, she still hasn't paid me for it.  There was a strong impulse to jerk off to the pictures, but I was able to restrain myself.  In reality, sometimes anything is preferable to writing, at least when it's non-fiction and requires a much more elaborate structure of bullshit than ordinary fiction.

I was going to have to stay away from the grandmother— the great-grandmother actually. She was a major distraction. On the other hand, there was no way I'd have anything to do with her, not that I haven't been with older women in my life. But I was never proud of it and thought fucking a 30+ year old in my teens was bad and a nearly 47 year old in my early twenties incrementally worse, but this would have been exponentially worse. Almost as bad as writing about a part of my life I didn't want to think about.

And she still owed me for the rolling papers and the Night Train!

It didn't take me long to realize that, aside from the grandmother who was almost certainly an active alcoholic and probably a pot head too—I'll refer to her as the grandmother or granny in spite that she's really a great-grandmother—that the kids were not as out of control as Glen said they were. They seemed quite normal.

They also all seemed smarter than Glen or Anne, well, the three younger ones anyway. Even though they talked with a deep south Mississippi accent, they still pronounced words correctly, very rarely saying things like 'y'all'—rhymes with small. They didn't use slang as much as I did when I was their age, though I've heard both Brittney and Lindsey say 'tripping' or 'trippin' once or twice, though I don't think they were talking about drugs. Sometimes 'yasss' instead of 'yes' and occasionally even 'dough' or 'doe' instead of 'though.' Usually their English is better than mine is with all the 'wows' and 'yeahs' that I crap out in ordinary conversation and I've never heard any of them say 'ain't,' a word that I used a lot at their age and still do, on occasion. Actually, I never used ain't until my second grade teacher said it was not a real word, was very improper English and that it should never be used. Only thing I really remember learning in the second grade.

The girls anyway even seemed polite for the most part and for some reason called me Uncle Fats rather than just Fats, though Billy usually just called me Uncle Fatty often without the Uncle. And, probably without actually trying to be politically correct, they rarely said the n-word, which is probably a good idea since they lived in an integrated neighborhood. Shortly after they moved here, Glen said they used the n-word all the time, even in front of their black neighbors, but I've never witnessed anything like that.

If I was going to go ahead with the Reality TV Show plan, I really had my work cut out for me on this. No one wants to watch a normal family. Most people want *The Osbornes*. Some might even want Kiss's bass player, the one with the big tongue, even though his children seemed relatively normal. But not many and after watching a few episodes of *Family Jewels*, I couldn't believe anyone watched such a lame show but I imagine some must, assuming it was on longer than the few episodes I saw. They want *Honey Boo Boo* or *Jersey Shore*.

I doubted they wanted the Morgan Bunch—though Morgan Monsters or Morgan Mess might work. Things like the *Brady Bunch* and *The Waltons* might have worked in the 70s and 80s, but not now.

We would have to play on the mother being a recovering crackhead on parole and maybe the family being reunited after the mother went to prison and the children were placed in foster homes. Hopefully it would not be investigated by half a dozen law enforcement and child welfare agencies. Actually, I'm surprised Anne's parole officer allowed me to rent a room in their house. Apparently it was only because I was "in recovery" for 16 years and the family really needed the money that she allowed it.

# Chapter 4 The Sell, or The Trailer Park Boys Meet Frankenstein

I decided I'd have to play Dr. Frankenstein and try to mold this zoo into a jungle of little monsters, at least while the cameras were running. I was hoping they'd be able to ad lib their parts with just an outline to a scenario. All four of the kids seemed bright, especially the three younger ones. Of course, if they could memorize lines, that would be much better. But the important thing was for them to appear to be acting normal and spontaneous. These are, of course, things I should have considered before moving here.

As far as I can tell, the main similarity they have with *Here Comes Honey Boo Boo*, in addition to being from the South, was that they made spaghetti sauce with ketchup, according to Glen anyway. With Anne's mother gone, maybe things will get better for them, spaghetti wise anyway.

There is one thing we could steal from that show, something that is probably more common down here than it is in the rest of the country. We could get one of the girls pregnant. Though we might want to save that for the second season. Or maybe end the first season with a cliff hanger, perhaps questioning or wondering if the baby's father was black or white or maybe throw an illegal immigrant into the mix of possible fathers.

It was mid-afternoon and I heard the television go on. I quietly opened my door to make sure it wasn't granny and saw that it was Lindsey, one of the thirteen year old twins. I thought Billy was the name of the boy and Brittney the name of the younger girl, but, at that point, I wasn't sure about either name. I only remembered Lindsey's name because she was just entering that age where she was starting to be fuckable--not that I would ever have entertained the idea of having sexual relations with someone that young! Of course, being the fat bastard that I am, it is almost a certainty that no one that young or even ten years older, would want to have sex with me. There are, of course, exceptions and I was glad I no longer drank, just in case she was one of those Lolita's who were always experimenting with, or sometimes just tormenting, older men. When I was drinking my moral character wouldn't have thought twice about avoiding temptation and back then the age of consent where I was living was 15, not that one year would probably have made a difference. Of course, by my late teens I drank too much to be considered functional in any sense and that kind of temptation rarely presented itself and only at times when I was straight and sober enough to ignore it.

Anyway, I decided to approach her and feel her up, I mean out, about a reality TV show. She had been channel surfing and didn't seem too engrossed with what she was watching. I sat down on the couch next to the easy chair she was sitting on.

"Ever want to be on a reality show?" I asked.

"Mean like survivor or big bother?"

"Something like that, but with fewer rules and where no one gets kicked off the island. Maybe a cross between *Jersey Shore, The Dirty South, Honey Boo Boo, The Osborne's* and, although not reality shows, *Curb Your Enthusiasm* and, Glen's favorite, *The Trailer Park Boys*."

"I don't think our family is exciting enough to keep anyone awake for more than the opening credits, if even that."

"Sometimes you have to make your own excitement. Or do something really controversial. Sometimes it might be scripted like *Duck Dynasty*, where someone has a task or something like that to do which they nearly always, or sometimes anyway, screw up."

At this point, she flipped the channel to one of the vhs or MTV channels that still played music videos and the Ann Lennox version of "A Whiter Shade of Pale" was playing which prompted Lindsey to say:

"You could call the show 'A Whiter Shade of Trash' maybe

with the unsaid joke implying that the real trash were the idiots watching the show." I actually liked that name, if not that particular cover of the song.

"Great show title! I guess that's true of a lot of things," I added, referring to her implied theme. I then remembered one of my college professors implying that the real monster in Mary Shelley's Frankenstein was the Doctor rather than his creation. As far as bringing out the little monsters in these children, I didn't think I'd be creating anything that wasn't already there. I still had to be careful. I didn't mind playing with puppets as long as no one saw me pulling the stings.

"Maybe we could end one episode with me or Brittney telling mom that one of us was pregnant and then say there's a 1 in 20 chance that the kid's father was black or a one in 40 chance that he was a Mexican," she said, which gave me a Frankenstein—déjà vu—moment. I was actually wondering if she was reading my mind, or, perhaps, my short term memory. "We could start the next episode by telling mom we were just joking." Which wouldn't have occurred to me, but which might work as a practical joke. Hell, it would work! And more importantly, she seemed willing to play along and even understanding that we would be playing as much as acting— manufacturing our own plots, problems and solutions.

"So do you think the others would be interested? It would probably have to be the whole family. Certainly the majority."

"Everybody wants their 15 minutes, at least when it doesn't include wearing handcuffs and going to prison."

Shortly afterwards, Brittney came in and Lindsey told her "I've been talking to Uncle Fats here about starting a Reality TV show and he seems to think it might work if the whole family is into it. Would you like to be on TV?"

"You don't have to convince me or Billy or Cinni or Mom or Glen or even Gram Gram," Brittney said. "But you will have to convince the bull dyke."

"The bull dyke?" I asked.

"Lucy Laroux," Brittney said. "I think she would have the final say."

"Who's that?" I asked.

"Mom's parole officer," Lindsey said. "She can be a real bitch sometimes. Mom and Glen both say she's a lizbian. Actually, I'm rather surprised she let you move it." Lesbian was one of the few words Lindsey didn't pronounce correctly.

"Mom and Glen call her Captain Carpet Muncher," Brittney said and started giggling.

"Not to her face," Lindsey added.

"Maybe we can come up with a nick name for her that's more flattering," I said. God help us if she's as bad as they say and then hears the nick name they have for her. Of course, I didn't add that I'd love to do an episode where the topic of discussion was eating pussy with maybe Glen telling Billy that to get a girl to like him, he should eat her pussy. Of course, the finale would be Billy saying she got really pissed because he BBQ'ed her pet cat. . . But I knew that would never be able to air in this country, not even on the premium channels. Back when I shared the house with Glen, all we ever talked about was eating pussy, eating ass, and football.

"You don't want to get her pissed off at your mom or Glen," I added. "She may take it out on the whole family, or at the very least, your mother."

At this point Billy came in, but headed straight toward his room. Lindsey went to talk to him but his door was locked. He came out of his room a half hour later, after masturbating I guessed, not that I mentioned that theory to either of the girls or Billy for that matter. By this point, we were discussing how the show had to exemplify family values with strong Christian themes. I suggested starting each episode with the whole family saying the Serenity Prayer and ending with one of them, usually one of the children including Cinni who was 18, kneeling by their bed saying their nightly prayers.  I thought that maybe the two older girls could nod their heads while praying as if they were listening to God (which could also be interpreted as simulating fellatio to any perverts watching the show).

Of course, it was between these prayer sessions that at least some in the family would raise all kinds of hell, the central idea being that kids will be kids.  We talked about improvising dialog along the lines of *Curb Your Enthusiasm*.

Billy must have heard us talking.

"You're crazy listening to this fat fuck," said the kid who was thinner than my by no means well endowed penis.

"Actually Billy, being the only available man on the show," I said, "you would be featured in just about every episode.  And the girls at school would be all over you."

"Mom's going to like that," Lindsey said.  "Her biggest fear in life is that Billy is gay.  'Not that there's anything wrong with that,'" Lindsey added the last line, quoting a favorite episode of *Seinfeld*.

"You don't have to tell her that you're boning a different girl every day.  Sometimes two or three at a time," I said, at which point both of the girls threw something at me—a small couch pillow and, I think, a pen.  "Being your mother, she'll know."  I didn't think that was something most women would be proud that their sons were doing, but Anne wasn't most women.  I wanted to add that all women become sluts around TV Stars but thought it was overkill and that the girls wouldn't agree.  And Billy was probably smart enough to know it wasn't true.

He seemed to be coming around until he heard Lindsey talk about the title for the show: "'A Whiter Shade of Trash,' like the Justin Beaver [huh?] song 'A Whiter Shade of Pale.'"

"No fuckin' way!  It would be a great name if the show was about Fats and Glen living in a trailer.  Glen might be white trash and maybe even Mom but we're an ordinary family and

I'm sick of being stereotyped as white trash just because were from the south.  Fatty's a lot more white trash than any of us and he's from New Jersey."

"The emphasis of the show would be on family values, not social status," I said, not sure he would understand the difference.  "Of course, there might be jokes about being white trash, but the audience would be smart enough to know that you were joking."  At this point, I thought it might take him a couple days to come around, but that he probably would, if only for the potential of becoming a pussy magnet or to attract other guys if that was his thing, or just to have his fifteen minutes of fame.

Brittney had a better idea.  She said: "We could just have us girls on the show and maybe show Glen sometimes sleeping on the couch and when uncle fats isn't directing, he can be our reverend or pastor."

Lindsey said: "I have a better idea. He could be one of those homophobic preachers who's in the closet and keeps getting caught in a pubic restrooms soliciting sex from undercover cops."

Billy found this hilarious.

"It's a great premise but it would never happen in real life. I'm not, nor have I ever been gay and I'm not planning on becoming gay anytime in the future."  I would never admit that I may have been ass fucked or, hopefully, if it actually happened, ass raped by that serial killer I used to travel with when I was around Billy's age.

"Maybe you could be one of moms old boyfriends," Lindsey said.

"Mom was never into fat guys," Billy said.

"Maybe I'm just an old friend of Glens who got conned into moving here to help with the rent?  Better yet, maybe I stay entirely behind the scenes."

As it turned out, Billy was in, but wanted no part of the

more white trash aspects of the show, including Lindsey's program title.  For the time being it would be called "The Morgan Family, their pets and sometimes Glen."

Anne, Cinni and Glen were also in.  Nobody even thought of asking granny, who, it turned out, was more willing to contribute in a negative sense—think ratings—then all the kids put together.  She even offered to flash her boobs during the opening credits which nobody else thought was a good idea.

# Chapter 5 The Dominatrix, or the Insidious meets the Insatiable

The hard part was over and now it was time for the very hard part. Anne brought me to see Lucy Laroux on her next scheduled visit to her parole officer. Although I was expecting her to be what the kids called a "bull dyke," I wasn't expecting her to be 6 feet tall or weighing around 180 pounds; and I had the feeling she had more weight in muscle than in fat.

"You really should tell me before you decide to bring a guest Anne," then she turned to me, smiled, held out her hand to shake and said "Lucille Laroux." She shook my hand a little more firmly than women usually do.

"And you're?" she asked.

"Forrest Beauregard, though most people call me Fats."

"Ah, the lodger. And you purpose for being here?"

"Anne thought you might want to meet me to discuss a plan I have about producing a pilot for a reality TV show about Anne's family."

"I'll make an appointment to see you. It will have to be after hours though, since you're not on parole. You're not right?"

"No. Other than a couple of minor disorderly conduct arrests and a DUI in the late 90s, I have a clean record."

"In that case, please wait outside in the outer waiting room."

Anne came out around 15 minutes later.

"She seemed interested in your relationship status and sexual orientation," she said on the drive home, between laughs. "Maybe she ain't as butch as we thought." Another laugh. "She asked me to tell you she made an appointment to see you tonight, at eight, preferably with the rest of us gone for a couple hours."

I'll skip as much of that night's meeting/sex romp with Lucy Laroux as I can. Lucy, who may be bi, though she denied it, was certainly into men though she was the most dominant woman that I ever had sex with as well as the most manipulative person I ever met.

We starting out on the living room couch talking about the project. She was constantly brushing her hand against me touching me here and there and within 5 minutes, she had my pants undone and my dick in her mouth. After I clearly started enjoying it, she suggested we move into higher gear in my bedroom. Somehow, she was able to undressed in seconds. She kneeled on the floor at the foot of my bed and started blowing me for the second time, but, just as I started to really relax and just let it happen, she lifted her head up and started jerking me off, quickly getting up and, while changing to the 69 position, she said:

"OK corporal carpet muncher, let's see what you got." At which point I realized she must have heard about the Captain Carpet Muncher nickname, didn't like it, and was taking it out on me. But I've heard drunken women say carpet muncher, probably referring to lesbians, with much worse inflections, so it really didn't bother me. (Afterwards though, I did become slightly offended, not so much at the Carpet Muncher title but rather at the Corporal designation, but at the time I threw myself into it. . . Actually, I like to think of *it* as something of an art. It's certainly something I'm a lot better at than I ever was at playing the guitar or writing.) She had my arms pinned under her shins so that I could only use my tongue and lips (I know, nose, chin, face were also tools that I could use and sometimes did, but didn't feel the need to or inclination). After half a minute she stopped jerking me, and lightly pressed her face against the shaft. I used all my preferred oral skills and techniques to bring her to climax as quickly as possible, but instead of reciprocating orally, she asked me which I preferred "Cowgirl or reverse cowgirl?"

And I made the mistake of saying: "Cowgirl, but I prefer to

be on top and I'd really like to finish in your mouth" hoping she would finish blowing me.

Instead, she rose up on her knees, turned around so that she faced me and partially kneeling, partially sitting without putting all of her weight on my chest, she said: "You'll have to eat me again if you want me to consider giving you a full service BJ. And don't stop until I tell you corporal."

She apparently finished three more times before she told me to stop at which point she rolled over onto her back while spreading her legs. Ordinarily, I'd use a rubber but by this time I figured if she had anything I could catch then I already had it and I figured she was on the pill or something since she didn't insist that I use protection. Even when I was on top, she still needed to be in control so that the missionary position quickly evolved into what's sometimes called the man trap where she intertwined her calf's inside my thighs which, although very enjoyable, can be too enjoyable. In this case, she finished, again, shortly before I did. My turn now to roll over. I would never admit it, but, once she allowed me to be on top, she was really good in bed.

At this point, I just wanted to zone out which she probably knew. She told me she wanted a cut of the profits, an associate producer credit under the name Liz Roux, that she would have to approve all the scenes that Anne was in and that Anne couldn't do anything that would violate her parole.

Around this time, the family came back and Glen came in the house and backed into the room and asked: "Would you mind if I closed the door so the rest of the family can come in the house?"

"Please," I said.

"And thank you," Lucy added.

We both got dressed and entered the living area. Glen quietly said to me: "Go to the bath room and look in the mirror. Quick!" As I should have realized, I had Lucy Laroux's DNA all over my face, chin and neck.  Parts of my chest too.

After I entered the living room, rather embarrassed, Anne said: "Miss Laroux said she had to leave, but that 'Corporal Carpet Muncher' will fill us in."

Feeling even more embarrassed, I started to explain the conditions, but before I could get more than a few syllables out, Brittney asked: "Is Uncle Fats a bull dyke?"

Something everyone found funny.  What I didn't find funny was Anne's remark about how now we know who's going to step up and blow any TV executives who need encouragement to get our show picked up.  No, not funny at all and hopefully not true. . .

# Chapter 6 The Pilot

I sent out queries to dozens different cable channels and the only one to express any interest was the *Guns and Ammo Sportsman* Channel as a possible lead in to one of their other shows. So I started work on a short treatment for the pilot.

1. Starts show the whole family saying the Serenity Prayer
2. Glen and kids go Hunting
3. Someone accidentally shoots a cow/pig/sheep/dog/cat? (Probably best not to shoot a person.)
4. Goes to firing range with targets with Obama in cross-hairs
5. Are kicked out of the range for mishandling firearms or nearly shooting one the other patrons
6. Glen gives lesson/lecture about firearm safety while kids play with weapons
7. Have a meal together where they talk about God and guns
8. End show with one of them saying their nightly prayers

A lot of it would have to be scripted, but I was hoping they could also ad lib most of the dialog.

We would have to video the hunting and target shooting scenes while Anne was a work. I'm sure Laroux would be pissed if she was around any guns, or God forbid, if she handled or shot one of them. Then again, maybe we could let her hunt with a bow and arrow.

Maybe when we have Glen give firearms safety speech and while the kids are all playing with the guns one of them accidentally be discharged a second after it was aimed at someones head. Make that a practical lesson in firearms safety. Then I started thinking that this could be dangerous, that the kid might actually shoot while the gun was aimed at someone's head. A thought passed through my head that maybe one of the kids could accidentally shoot Laroux but I refused to entertain it thinking maybe she'd finally finish that blow job if the show becomes a hit—better her than granny!

Maybe it would be better if we didn't shoot a cow, dog, etc. or get kicked off the firing range. Show that the kids can handle firearms responsibly. For controversy, we still had the Obama targets. Only we had to explain that we were targeting him because he's a liberal—not because he's black! We don't want anyone to think that the kids are racist—even if they were. Or not too racist anyway. Racism is not a family value that we would want to perpetuate, in my opinion anyway. I'm sure there is a large racist audience, but I doubted their demographics were rated by Nealsons. Obama would be targeted because he was the country's worst president. I also didn't want to disparage his perceived religion, if only because I didn't want Islamic extremist to target us or our show.

As with writing my book about the serial killer, I was finding it harder write about this family. Sad to say, but they were just too common. Not that Honey Boo Boo was all that crazy, though they did seem to epitomize white trash, something that probably only Billy seemed aware enough to be ashamed of the label. For the second show, I'd see if Billy would be willing to take on the affect of a singer or a rapper.

For the hunting scenes in the pilot I would make sure all the guns were unloaded. Check and check again, having learned not quite the hard way that unloaded firearms can kill when I accidentally put a bullet through a window and probably somewhere in the siding or walls of a neighbor's house. I used the term not quite the hard way because no one, that I know of anyway, got wounded or killed. Fortunately the unloaded .22 revolver was loaded with .22 shorts so I doubt if it went through the siding and both sides of the wall and into the house itself, assuming it didn't hit a window.

I only had four shoulder weapons so I thought I'd let Cinni

shoot the 12 gauge Pump Shotgun, Billy have the 12 gauge single shot shotgun, Lindsey could weld the Chinese made AK-47—which, of course, everyone wanted to play with—and Brittney a .22 rifle.

Laroux, actually earning her AP title, knew someone who would allow us to go wild boar hunting on their property. (What I didn't know was that I would have to pay for this information by taking her our to dinner.  Fortunately, she wasn't very high maintenance when it came to dining and didn't mind Popeyes.  Of course, her idea of desert, for me anyway was another B&D session, the bondage consisting of her kneeling on my upper arms and pinning them down while I was eating at the Y.)

Getting someone who would let us boar hunt on their property was a stroke of luck, since it would be a few months before hunting season began for anything big anyway.  At some point I planned to let them all fire the AK-47, though probably no more than 5 rounds each—I only had around forty rounds.

We left Anne at home for our first video project.  I managed to video the kids shooting at what will hopefully appear to be a moving animal once we can get some video of something moving.  Glen and the kids made so much noise talking and tromping around that I figured it would scare away any wild boars that weren't deaf.

Our next stop was an indoor firing range in a neighboring town east of Bay St. Louis.  We had to get special permission to allow more than two people on the range at one time and Glen had to pretend to be the kids father rather than stepfather.  They probably only went along with it because they thought I would be good publicity.

Although I would later claim I bought the targets from someone outside, I actually printed them that morning on my Ink Jet printer.  I used a standard picture of Obama within a series of circles centering on the bridge of his nose.  I wasn't really sure if this was a good idea.  My motivation was ratings, not politics.  Of course, I didn't take into account that the kids were raised in an environment where Obama might actually— no, probably was—the Antichrist.  Hell, I didn't actually even believe Obama was a Muslim, though I pretended I did. Although I have my own spiritual beliefs, as far as this show was concerned, all I really believed in was ratings.  It was just good—bad—whatever luck that the two women in the booth next to ours were black and offended enough by our target to take issue with it.

"Who the fuck you think you're shooting at?" one of the women asked.

"The Antichrist!" Brittney said, whose turn hadn't come yet.  Her ears, even wearing ear protection, were good enough to actually hear the woman's question.  We were all, of course, wearing ear protection so most of us missed the brief exchange. Fortunately my sound equipment recorded it.

At this point I tried to get them to sign a waver to appear on our show, but they probably thought it was something to do with the KKK and refused to sign, perhaps thinking we wanted their names and addresses for some nefarious purpose.  I told them we were shooting a Reality TV show and they might appear on it anyway, but they wouldn't get paid or credited if they didn't sign the wavers.  Actually they wouldn't get paid even if they did sign the waver, but their names might appear in the closing credits.

"You can take your show and shove it up your fat ass along with your clipboard and your wavers," said the second black woman.  Both, apparently, were New Orleans police officers.

Unfortunately the kids stayed out of it and Glen only laughed adding "I told you not to use those targets."

At this point one of the "range officers" came over to find out what the problem was, but he wouldn't sign a waver either. When he heard about the Obama targets he wasn't very sympathetic to us saying we should "use different targets or leave."

None of the kids nor Glen wanted to escalate things.   I asked Glen to hold the camera for a moment and then I offered the two woman $10 each if, after a count down of ten to zero, they would start chanting "No justice, no peace!" but instead of accepting my money, one of them punched me in the eye and the other kicked me in the right shinbone.   Now the range officer decided to get into it with me and he grabbed me from behind and put me in half nelson and escorted me off the range. Since the range officer was 3 or 4 inches shorter than me, I was walking, almost staggering, in a very uncomfortable position, with my back, neck and head bent backwards at an uncomfortable angle.   Glen was able to video most of what followed, but mainly the targets would make it on the pilot.

Next Glen conducted a series of personal interviews with the kids hi-lighting what they learned about hunting, shooting and gun safety.   The oldest of the girls learned never to aim a gun at someone.   The second oldest to never assume a gun was empty.   And the youngest learned, after around seven takes, "never to shoot at pictures of Obama around African Americans—not that I got a chance to shoot."   Billy would sum things up by saying that he wished he "had bagged a wild boar because, white or black, we can all agree that everyone loves bacon!"

The following Thursday, when both Anne and Glen had the day off, we shot the family dinner scene.   This was a complete rip off of how Duck Dynasty used to sometimes end their shows only with more emphasis on the children, with the adults mainly just answering questions and acting sanctimonious. Since this was a guns episode, one of the questions would be "If Jesus was alive today, what kind of gun would he carry?" and "Would he need a concealed carry permit?"   Granny could proclaim: "it doesn't matter what kind of shooting irons Jesus uses, just make sure He ain't using them on you." Here Glen or Anne could exclaim that "Jesus might not even need a gun. He could summon ten thousand Angels to do his bidding, though in your case Billy, that might be a little overkill."

In the final take, granny changed "shooting irons" to "roscoe," which I had always thought was a (usually large) penis and Glen changed "Jesus" to "God" and "in your case Billy," to "in some cases." The kids all had their lines down pat and improvised a few minutes of general discussion that could be added to the pilot. I guess they figured that if Laroux could get an associate producer title just for granting permission to make the pilot, then they could get one too by providing additional dialog. This was OK with me as long as they didn't expect more money.

Only Cinni and Brittney would let me video them saying their nightly prayers. Cinni prayed that her boyfriend get a better job so she could marry him and quit her job. Brittney thanked Jesus for all the blessings he had bestowed on her, and her family and asked that next time they go to the firing range that she "get a chance to shoot at Obama." I decided I'd keep Cinni's prayer for (slightly possible) later use, and use Brittney's for the final scene before the closing credits. I had planned to edit out the "at Obama" part but never got around to it, though I worked for a few days digitally splicing the pilot together.

For a show title we finally settled on "The Morgan Family Rules!!!" with the three exclamation marks. Glen would later expound that the exclamation marks implied: "Rules to live by as in good common sense, Rules to be obeyed such as the 10 commandments and laws not created by liberals, and, finally, in Rules as in being really cool!" After hearing this I wanted to remove a couple exclamation marks, but was too lazy to redo the title logo.

During the opening we showed a still picture of all the

Christmas presents the kids got this year, followed and short clips of Billy playing one of my guitars, Cinni getting out of the car, Lindsey riding her bike and looking like she was crashing into the side of a building, Brittney sneaking a piece of cake from the refrigerator, Anne cooking hamburgers, Granny playing video games on an X Box and finally Glen taking a nap on the couch. I thought of adding the two dogs, Princess and Dallas, but was not able to capture any decent footage of them.

I recycled a punk song I wrote when I was in my teens, originally titled Roundhouse Turntable. I changed the lyrics of the first verse from "I want to get in the little bitches pants" to "I want to see into the Morgan family life" repeated 8 times. I slowed it down from 216 beats per minute to around 138 BPM and didn't use the second verse, which was the same as the first, the third verse, "I think this song is getting repetitious," or the fourth verse, "I want to cum in the little bitches mouth," all lines repeated 8 times. For the closing, I was going to rewrite another song I wrote from that period originally called "Filet Fellatrix," but remembered that they nearly always cut the sound during the ending credits to announce other programs on the network and left the closing with just Glen and me improvising.

In the closing credits I listed myself as director and producer, Arthur as Executive Producer, Laroux and all the kids as Associate Producers. I ended the credits with: "*The Morgan Family Rules!!!* Copyright © MMXIV by Fats Beauregard and the Morgan-Carter Family, All rights reserved." Since the show didn't air until 2015, I later changed the copyright to MMXV.

It took more than an hour to upload the pilot to the G&A Sportsman's channel website. I emailed my contact there the file name as soon as the upload was completed.

I was also supposed to show the finished pilot to Laroux, or at the very least, the scenes with Anne in it before submitting it. I decided against it to avoid another muff diving session not yet realizing that sometimes going downtown was unavoidable.

At this point I was going to think positively and start working on a second episode. I realized that the pilot probably wouldn't "air" until the Spring or Summer or, more likely, the following Fall, but was determined to get a few made. I had originally thought about the family forming a Cowsills, Jackson 5, Osmond Brothers or Partridge Family style group, but I didn't really know if any of them could sing or play a musical instrument, other than Glen who was OK on guitar.

Glen had pawned his guitar along with his Laptop and I had vowed never to let him play my Telecaster after the terrible thing he said about Telecasters, that: "they're mainly only used in country music." I did let Billy play it, and once or twice my SG, but he was as bad at learning chord names as Glen was and I had little hope of turning him into a competent musician. I was too lazy to bring my amplifier into the living room and never let the younger girls in my room fearing they might try to jump me and force themselves on me and the oldest girl wasn't interested in learning the guitar.

I would really have to think about this. I went to sleep that night unsure about the next step for The Morgan Family Rules!!!

# Chapter 7 "My Wiggaz"

The following morning I had another brainstorm and asked Billy before he left for school if he'd be interested in rapping in the next episode.

"Hell no, that's ghetto music. The only thing I hate more than rap is like classical and country music. I even like that heavy metal glam rock shit that Glen likes more than rap."

"Yeah but with rap you don't have to sing or have a great voice, just a feeling for rhythm and tempo. And think of it this way, you'd be the focus of, no, the *star* of the whole episode. And you'd only have to learn one or two rap songs. Three at the most. There wouldn't be any free styling or anything like that."

"I'll think about it," he said.

That day I wrote a parody of DMX's "My Niggaz" called "My Wiggaz." After waiting several weeks for Billy to agree to it, I decided if Billy wasn't going to do it, probably Cinni, Lindsey, or Brittney would.

After being discouraged before Billy finally agreed to do it, I had written the following verse, which would have been rapped by one of the girls:

My brother Billy says he's a pimp (My Wiggaz)
in reality he only a wimp  (My Wiggaz)
got a dick no bigger than a shrimp (My Wiggaz)
a wimp  (My Wiggaz)
a shrimp  (My Wiggaz)

I added the "My Wiggaz" at the end of each line instead of the beginning and put together an 8 bar loop on my keyboard and then recorded it adding seven tracks of me saying "My Wiggaz." If we were actually going to be making a real recording, I would have done a much more professional job, probably getting the kids, as well as Anne, Glen and Granny to pitch in on the "My Wiggaz" part. But right now, I just wanted to have something that he could practice with.

He read the rap and started laughing. Finally, he paused and said: "This is bull shit. Like really I doubt if I could do it with the straight face."

"No ones going to believe those things about your sisters, it's just supposed to sound like a white kid attempting to sound like a gangster rapper."

"It's you being a great man that's the real bull shit. And I ain't a wigger, I've never even met one. I don't think there are any in Mississippi. Not in Waveland, the Kill or Bay St. Louis anyway. Or at least no one who has the bad enough sense to admit it."

"Think of it as just a silly phase you're going through. At the end of the episode we can have granny pray for you to come to your senses and we can try having you and/or one of your sisters become a Christian Heavy Metal singers in another episode."

"I'll give it a try. Let me read through it a few more times," he said, adding, contemptuously, "great man, what of load of shit!"

When he was ready I started the looper connected to my amplifier.

my big sista she likes to fuck (My Wiggaz)
when she's raggin' it she gives good suck (My Wiggaz)
got no bling to give her you got no luck (My Wiggaz)
she fucks (My Wiggaz)
and fucks (My Wiggaz)
my twin sista she likes to steal (My Wiggaz)
has a script for meds that she will deal (My Wiggaz)
has sistas trick money hid in her heal (My Wiggaz)
she steals (My Wiggaz)
she steals (My Wiggaz)

my old granny she like to drink (My Wiggaz)
got a meth lab hid under the sink (My Wiggaz)
she tweaks shits herself and she stinks (My Wiggaz)
she drinks (My Wiggaz)
and stinks (My Wiggaz)
my uncle Fatty is a great man (My Wiggaz)
he helps us as no other can (My Wiggaz)
he's always there to give us a han' (My Wiggaz)
a great heart (My Wiggaz)
and he's smart (My Wiggaz)
my mom wants me to go to school (My Wiggaz)
and wants me to follow the rules (My Wiggaz)
she must think i some kind of fool (My Wiggaz)
go to school? (My Wiggaz)
hell no fool! (My Wiggaz)
my step dad comes home and he sleeps (My Wiggaz)
he masturbates, smokes and he sleeps (My Wiggaz)
he feeds his dog and goes to sleep (My Wiggaz)
he sleeps (My Wiggaz)
and sleeps (My Wiggaz)
my younga sista she's got big tits (My Wiggaz)
i says again she's got big tits (My Wiggaz)
did i tell you that she's got big tits (My Wiggaz)
big tits (My Wiggaz)

"Enough," Anne exclaimed.

"Big t..." Billy stopped rapping though the DMX style "My Wiggaz" remix soundtrack continued playing in the background.

"Anne, your son is an extremely talented rapper" I said hoping she'd believe anything positive I said about her kids, even though she hated rap as much as Glen's or my grand parents hated heavy metal. "He can make the family a lot of money.

"We also need a hook for the reality show," I continued as "My Wiggaz" still played. "Just going out and shooting guns and saying like 'if it God's will, then Obama should be shot' is not enough to get us ratings on even the *Guns and Ammo* network. We need to bring in a mainstream audience and Billy's rapping will do that just as Bud Bundy's rapping on *Married with Children* saved that show after everyone thought it had jumped the shark and kept it on the air for four or five more years."

"I can't have him saying the terrible things he's saying about his sisters," she said, a little less angry now. "We are a God fearing Christian family after all."

"Yes, but this is what brings the family values into the show. The juxtaposition between what Billy is rapping about or saying," I paused for effect, "say about Cinni's perceived sex life, and the actuality about what a sweet wholesome gal that she really is. And, of course, no one would believe granny was a tweaker. She's too fat to be a meth head. The only truth in the rap is when he's talking about Glen."

By this time someone had turned off the DMX remix on my looper, but I didn't notice who, just that it was off. We were still recording video though. That was the important thing.

"Glen doesn't masturbate! And he shouldn't be talking about Brittney's breast. She's only ten years old, for heaven's sake!"

"Don't take the Lord's name in vain!" Granny said while Brittney simultaneously said: "I'm eleven! An' you're just jealous 'cause my tits are bigger than yours!"

"We're just trying to add an edge of coolness to Glen. Of course he doesn't jer- masturbate, but he does sleep a lot. Saying he masturbates makes him look like a rebel rather than some poor slob who has sex with his wife, smokes a cigarette and then goes to sleep." I doubt if sex has ever been as free and easily available that one would consider masturbating as an act of rebellion, but sometimes the more noise you make the easier it is to distract someone. "If you really want, Billy can rap about Glen's sex life. But it would have to be something cool like having sex on a boat, or on the kitchen table or in the parking lot of the Superdome after a Saints game. Not some--"

"You and Glen had sex of the kitchen table?" Billy asked.

"That's none of your business," Anne said. By this time, she had forgotten about red lighting "My Wiggaz" so that, for all intents and purposes, it was on.

"Now we really need to plan out the next episode. Maybe with some moral teachings or lessons," changing things to religion always refocused them.

"How about if I asked why did the jews killed Jesus?" Brittney asked.

"Great!" I said. "Maybe we can bring it into the 21st century by redefining the actual Jews who killed Jesus not so much by their religion but by the fact that they were liberals. That we shouldn't blame conservative Jews, if there are any, just the liberal Jews and, all other liberals too?" Yeah, that's the ticket, I thought, thinking maybe, we might even get mentioned on Fox News.

"It was the Romans who killed--" Lindsey tried to say.

"I don't know about that" Anne said, ignoring the points both Lindsey and I were trying to make. "I was always told it was the Jews who killed Christ."

"Of course it was the Jews," I said. "But back then, Jews were all liberals. I mean, who else, other than a liberal would take issue about JC healing people on Sunday? Back then they only had one day weekends and no paid vacations. If the liberals had their way, we have 3 or 4 day weekends and 6 week vacations and nothing would ever get done and only immigrants would be working and you and Glen would lose your jobs."

"I don't know about this. And don't forget, Glen's a liberal and we try not to hold it against him."

"He's also a Cowboys fan, but we don't hold that against him either.  In any case, it would just be a theory we would bring up for discussion, and here, we have to think Ratings!"

"One of us can bring up the theory," Billy said.

"Great thinking!" I said, knowing Anne wouldn't.  "And anyway, it's just a sound byte.  Something to feed our viewers hoping they will buy into it.  Like putting pictures of Obama on targets.  Of course, none of us wants to shoot Obama," I wasn't really sure about this, but we had to at least make viewers think that the family wasn't really that crazy.  "We're just being controversial while, at the same time, trying to appear like we are just being spontaneous.  That's why we don't rehearse, so it looks spontaneous.  We just think of what we're going to say and then follow through.  We just say what's on our mind."

"I was thinking maybe talking about Doggie and Kitty Heaven," Brittney said.  "Maybe we could blame the liberals for keeping Dogs and Cats out of heaven?"

"Anyone want to field that?"

"Anyone?"

Heads shake and eyes get averted. . .

"Actually, it's probably a pretty damn good idea," I said, actually thinking it was pretty stupid.  "Someone could ask that question and maybe someone else could mention that's liberals have no real power in heaven, but that they tell us here on earth that God hates Cats and Dogs so much that He won't allow them in heaven and segregates departed pets in separate heavens.  But that it's really just a liberal conspiracy to turn people away from God.

"We can then expound upon this by saying there's no biblical proof that pets can't go to heaven and then Glen can mention a Twilight Zone episode where Heaven wouldn't be heaven if it didn't allow dogs.  The important thing is we blame the liberals."

"I don't understand why liberals want to keep dogs out of heaven," Lindsey said.

"Hell," Billy said, "if liberals had their way they'd keep guns out of heaven too."

I doubted there was any truth to this, but added: "You can be sure liberals won't be able to revoke the second amendment in heaven like they want to do in America."

While I was planning the next episode, I kept checking my email for a response from the Guns and Ammo channel, but it would be several days before they replied and their answer was NO! I didn't let that discourage me. There were thousands of other channels, or so it seemed, and I was sure somewhere one of them would be willing to air out show.

I was thinking about some of the religious channels when Glen told me that his old sponsor from Desert Center, California, was involved in the Patriot Second Amendment Channel and he gave me his email address, but asked me not to mention him. Being careful not to not mention Glen, I sent him an email to see if he'd be interested is seeing the pilot. I embedded a picture in the email of the whole Carter-Morgan family, making sure Glen stood out in the picture. I explained how pro-second amendment the family was: That they loved hunting and shooting.

I wasn't expecting anything, but Arch Renoir emailed me back within an hour and included a link to upload the pilot, and instructions. I quickly uploaded the file, or started the upload process anyway, and told everyone to keep their fingers crossed.

They didn't reply back to us until the second week of February. They offered us $50,000 per episode for 8 episodes including the pilot, which they said would air on Thursday, March 19, with a new episode each succeeding week on

Thursdays.   They wanted four complete episodes before premiering the pilot so we had around 5 weeks to finish three more episodes and we had already had recorded at least part of the second episode.

This was a lot less money than I was expecting, not that I expected a lot.  Although I was upset about it, when I brought it to them they seemed very happy about it.   If split evenly, everyone including Granny, Laroux, Arthur and me could get $5000 an episode, but I would try to negotiate so that Granny and Laroux only got $2000, so that we would have $6000 to cover expenses, hire a crew, etc.   If it was picked up for a second season, the amount would go up to $100,000 per episode for 12 to 24 episodes.

Before excepting any money, we formed a corporation giving everyone involved 5 shares, expect for Granny who really only appeared in the Super and the morning prayer scenes.  And, of course, Laroux, who was really just shaking us down.   But she was an officer of the criminal justice system and Anne was in the system, so there wasn't much we could do. Laroux also insisted that the treasurer of the corporation have some kind of accounting experience.   Since Arthur and me were the only ones who to took accounting in college, and Arthur claimed he was too busy to be treasurer, I came closest to matching that criteria.   She had no objection to Glen president,   Anne vice-president, Cinni secretary and me treasurer.

According to Glen, the kids didn't want me getting the same share that they were getting, but Glen and Anne were able to explain that I was doing most of the work, even though they didn't always like what I was doing.  Not sure if they pointed out that the whole show was my idea and that they weren't famous enough to deserve diva money.

When all the paper work was done I tried to get everyone to sign the necessary papers.  Anne had to co-sign the contracts of the three younger children.  The grandmother signed without a problem, as did Arthur, who financed us originally and now didn't have to do anything except collect his "dividends." Laroux was the only problem.   She didn't care about the amount she was getting, but she wanted to sign the paper Liz Roux, her associate producer name.   I gave in rather than getting drawn into another B&D Yodeling in the Valley session and had her papers rewritten with her Cruising, I mean Associate Producer, Name on them.   I don't know if it was legal, but I figured—hoped—it was her problem if it wasn't.

Brittney suggested that the two dogs should get shares since they were onscreen 'actors' but when I suggested that it would come out of her share, she gave up the idea.

It should be mentioned that most of the proceeds for the three younger kids would be deposited in trust funds for them, to be used for their college education, etc.  The oldest daughter went on half paid leave from work during the time we would be shooting the next seven episodes.  She would get half pay on the condition that she wore her Crazy Burger uniform for at least 50% of the time she appeared in each episode.  Glen and Anne would hang onto their jobs, Anne because it was a condition of her parole that she be employed and Glen because he didn't think the show would be successful.

# Chapter 8 B Street Billy

We began the second episode with the Serenity Prayer, as usual. Then Granny said: "I hope its just a phase you're going through Billy, because I find it impossible to accept that racket you're making."

"Billy's going to be the next Eminem," Lindsey said.

"More likely the next Vanilla Ice," Cinni said, adding: "Word to your Mother."

"I rather think of myself as a light skinned 2Pac. I got some serious things to say."

"You could be like Kayne West," Lindsey said. "The voice of our generation."

"Maybe you could become a recovering gay fish like Kayne," Brittney said, alluding to a recent *South Park* episode.

"No, he's gonna be himself," Glen said. Here he ad libbed: "I think he should do Jay Z's '99 Problems' changing only nig, uh, the n-word, to wigger."

"Wigga fool!" Billy said. "Wigger is an insulting, derogatory, ethnic slur."

There was more to this that he forgot to add, but it was at the wrong time, the whole line was meant to be said after Brittney was supposed to ask Billy *"Was up wigger?"* He got the important point out that wigger was a nasty offensive word, while wigga was almost a term of endearment among family, close friends, conspirators, even under the right set of circumstances, compatriots. At least I hoped our audience would be smart enough to figure it out, and if not, that they might get a laugh out of it. In any case his rapping was probably just going to be a phase he was going through.

"Wait until we record my version of 'My Wiggaz' before offering other rap songs. I've already decided that if it doesn't get over 5000 downloads within a week after the episode it's in airs, then I'm not going to do any more rapping and go back to my true love."

"Masturbating?" Brittney ad libbed.

Billy, quite visibly blushing, said: "What I really like would probably be d'fined as Grunge Metal; sort of a cross between all the good shit, sorry, I mean good crap mom use' to listen to when we were kids, but none of the bad shit like Britnney Spears or Suck Asylum."

"You don't like *Runaway Train?*" Anne asked.

"That's the one thing I can think of that ever made me want to run away from home, that and maybe *Misery* and Myanus Oralsex's *Ironic.*"

"Don't call her that!. She's a great singer, a poet really!"

"Maybe I'd let her go down on me in a theater if I was as old as Glen or Fatty, maybe even on an elevator a," he paused here though I wasn't sure if it was for effect or he was thinking what to say next, "in a parking lot or the driveway!"

Anne started toward him with her fists clenched, starting to bring them up, when Glen grabbed her around the waste and said: "Cut!" and when I kept recording, he said "Cut, cut, CUT!" the last time shouting it!

[Not that it necessarily means anything to what was currently being discussed, but one of the kids, Glen never told me which, busted Anne giving Glen a blow job in Anne's driveway shortly after they first hooked up. Back then she was living in a much smaller house and slept in the living room where she, and later Glen, had very little privacy.]

I pressed a button putting on the video camera putting it in its widest screen mode, and another that changed it to its highest resolution, closed the side panel of the video recorder, somehow forgetting to actually turn it off.

They were all looking at me, so I said: "Lets take ten, try to calm down."

At this point, all three or Anne's daughters started ganging up on Billy, telling him that he: "Shouldn't talk to his mother that way," and "shouldn't use such awful language" and shouldn't this and shouldn't that.

Then Glen said the worst comment of them all, "He wouldn't know what a blow job was even if he had a dick in his mouth."

"Y'all just jealous 'cause I'm the only one here with any real star potential," Billy said, and then added: "Tell them Uncle Fatty."

Which brought laughs and giggles to most of them, and a few eye rolls in disbelief.

"You believe that fat fuck?" Anne asked. "He's told that to all of us, probably even Princess, Dallas and even Laroux. We only let him pretend to manipulate us because we want our 15 minutes, same as you do."

"That's true Billy," I said, nodding, "The rest of the family is talented too. They may not have your rapping abil--"

"Cut the shit Fats!" Anne said, "Vanilla Ice was a more talented rapper than Billy. And he could at least dance!"

"Fatty said real men don't dance, only gays do. Real men might rhymingly strut their shit, but that's attitude, not dancing."

"Rhythmically strut their shit," I corrected Billy. Then, being the voice of reason, I suggested: "Maybe we could all go back to our separate corners."

Other than the dialog concerning me and anything I said, which had no valid reason for appearing on the show, this was a lot better than I ever hoped things would get. This was a lot crazier than *Duck Dynasty* or even going alligator hunting with *Swamp People* or the *Here Comes Honey Boo Boo* family and that was, after all, the reason I moved in with them. Now I would just have to play the peacemaker so that they wouldn't kick me out. Although we were contractually committed to making seven more episodes, and I would still get my cut, there had to be something in the shows that people would want to watch. Conflict was good, but it was better when it was directed at something external. This is a good Christian God and Gun loving family, the best of America, or so I wanted our target audience to believe and I didn't want people thinking they were going to start shooting each other.

Fortunately, for me anyway, Granny, the liberal of the family, decided to expound on Glen's last comment saying: "If you do find yourself with a dick in your mouth Billy, be sure to spit out the semen. According to the voice of my generation, the great Anita Bryant, semen is the fruit of the forbidden tree of life, and those who drink it are condemned to hell. That's why God hates fags so much."

I was hoping this would start a discussion about the relative virtues of spitting verses swallowing, but Anne shouted:

"Enough Gram!  I don't want to hear another word about anything to do with that topic."

Apparently Granny, already tipsy, and perhaps angry at Billy for labeling her a meth head, had to get her last word.  As she stood in the kitchen door leading out to the side of the house near her trailer, she said, loud enough to be heard by half the neighbors on the block: "I haven't swallowed a load since Jimmy Carter was President, praise Jesus, and that's more important than you're stupid rap songs you little cocksucker!"

We all just shook our heads, some of us snickering.  I tried making eye contact with Cinni, to see in the comment offended her, but she just seemed amused.  I didn't think I would ever have any chance of sticking it to her, but she was the only one who was both available and fuckable, legally speaking anyway. Part of me wanted to believe that if she ever hook up with me for a quickie, that she'd let me finish in her mouth.  Of course, she was so good-looking that I'd go down on her just, as the girls I grew up with would always say to prove their point, because.

"If Granny acted like this while we were recording," I said, "I'd definitely want to give her a larger share."

"She could have her own tee-shirt made," Billy said, "with the caption 'I spit for Jesus.'"

This got a laugh out of Cinni, Glen and me, though Anne was clearly angry while Lindsey and Brittney were confused.

"I'm cool with it if you want to call it a day," I said. "We got some good footage. Too bad the best lines were said while the video camera was off," I lied.

"I would take the whole year off if I could," Anne said. "If y'all want to keep filming, you can do it without me. I got to work this afternoon and could use a few more hours sleep."

After Anne left, I said: "If you're serious about uploading 'My Wiggaz' we should have at least two more raps ready so we can release a CD single."

"No one buy's CD's anymore," Billy said.

"True, but you won't get any royalties from downloads. Maybe half a cent on the dollar. If you're lucky, a penny or two. Most of the royalties go to the writers, but they probably make no more than four or five cents—if they're lucky."

"So you get all the royalties? That ain't fair!"

"No, DMX does, or whoever wrote it. It's already been copyrighted. We can't really add to it. Our version would be considered a parody. I don't make the rules and I can't change the copyright laws. If you want, you can write something or we can write something together and split the royalties 50/50."

"Fifty percent of nothing is nothing," Cinni said.

"I can't allow myself to be that negative. Just a few months ago, the whole idea of the Carter-Morgan family having a reality show didn't even exist. We had to believe in the idea to bring it to fruition. The odds are against the show being really successful, but that's true for every network and cable show too."

"So I have a better chance of being a rap star?" Billy asked.

"We have to create some kind of magic or a trend or something," I said to the delusional kid. "First you need a rap name Uzi Bill or Billy Tech 9.   Something people will remember.

"I got one," Brittney said. "How about Bay Saint Billy."

"I got a better one," Lindsey said. "The GPS version: Bay Street Billy.  Better yet, B Street Billy."

Billy actually liked the name B Street Billy.

Cinni had to go to work and Glen join Anne.  It took the four of us around an hour to write the following masterpiece:

Some Wiggaz think I'm the B. Street Louis clown
But my nine and me got ta mow some Wiggaz down
I hip and I hop and rap all over the bay
And I'll drop all you mothers who get into my way.

The funeral director gives me a dividend
A piece of the action for the bodies I send
The hearse drives by another message is sent
You mess with B Street Billy you got no time to repent

I'm the King. . , I'm the Bay Saint Louis King
I'm everything, cause I'm the Bay Saint Louis King
I rock and roll and for this crown I sol' my soul
Cause I'm the king and that is everything.

Most Wiggaz know I'm the B Street Louis King
And the hos all love me and they love to wax my thing
They take all I can give and more trying to appease
And then cry-cry-cry for more of me and drop down to
their knees.

I'm the King, I'm the Bay Saint Louis King
I'm everything, cause I'm the Bay Saint Louis King
I rock and roll and for this crown I sol' my soul
Cause I'm the king and that is everything.

I didn't particularly like it, but I wrote as much of it as everyone else, so ordinarily we'd each get a songwriting credit, though to appease Billy, I gave him my credit and any royalties I might earn from it—not that I was expecting any. Officially, "Bay Saint Louis King" was written by Billy, Lindsey and Brittney Morgan. I figured we could end the episode with it and then split the screen showing Granny praying that he outgrow this fad and maybe as an extra "and please don't let him swallow any semen" using captions showing what she was praying even though I wasn't sure if scripting prayers was a good idea. Then again, I had no problem with Cinni simulating fellatio while praying—not that I was able to get her to go along with it. She pretended to be disgusted by the idea.

After videoing it, everyone else was done for the day and I went to my room and edited the video. It took several hours but I got most of it down. I had to do a lot of panning for shots after Glen said CUT, but it was worth it. I even captured the audio of Granny's parting comments. They would probably be pretty pissed when they saw the episode when it aired, but until then they would know nothing of it. And, if I didn't include the part where Glen said "Cut," maybe they'd forget.

The next day we videoed the B Street Louis rap by B Street Billy and his Posse. To add a little something different to it, I had the girls rap along with Billy for the last four syllables of each line, getting even Cinni to take part. I actually thought it sounded pretty good and it was definitely different. It was great to have all four kid involved in the video, three participating in the creation process.

The idea of non urban kids in Mississippi being Wiggaz was ludicrous as was the idea of a skinny wimpy kid like Billy pretending to be a gangster rapper. But it's also controversial, which is the main thing. And, as long as it's perceived as a passing phase, like say a coked up ultra-right wing christian congressman getting caught with a dick in his mouth, then all will be forgiven as long as he repents.   And, unlike the congressman, Billy and the girls won't have to pray the gay away.  They'll just go on to something new like Grunge Metal or Christian Punk Rock.

Hell, maybe in one episode we'll get Billy or one of the girls to shave their head and get into some kind of neo-nazi or white supremacist rock.  Then again, that might get more than just the liberals all crazy and might actually anger the network's sponsors.

Except for the closing prayer, I had that episode put together nicely, with the somewhat shorter one where the rap fight scene ended when Glen said 'cut' ready in case anyone wanted to see it before it aired.

# Chapter 9 Mardi Gras Mistakes

Someone from the Patriot Channel called me and asked if we were considering doing a Morgan Family Mardi Gras episode and said if we were going to, then he would have a few thousand plastic Doubloons made in various colors with Morgan Family Rules and, in a smaller font size, (coming this spring) on one side and the Channels official new name: *American Patriot God and Gun Channel* and, again in much smaller font, premiering Thursday, March 19, 2015 on the other side. When I said that I was pretty sure something could be arranged, they had them made and Fed Ex Next Day Air shipped to us. Someone had made a mistake and instead of shipping a few thousand, they shipped a few thousand of each of five colors, Purple, Gold, Silver, Green and Blue.

I thought I was going to have to hire people to throw these around figuring the actual Krewes on the floats wouldn't, but then I thought maybe I could just hire one person to hand them out to people to throw, so they'd have something to do. The point was to throw them over the floats, or, in the French Quarter, over the Marchers to the people on the other side. This was, of course, advertising at its crudest. But what can you expect from a White Trash Killbilly family. But we would give them out anyway we could even if it was illegal.

The following weekend was the last weekend of Mardi Gras. I secured permission to take the kids to New Orleans to hopefully get enough footage for the third episode. Cinni got one of her old boyfriends, along with a friend of his, as additional cameramen for the day. They were actually willing to work for minimum wage and wait to be paid until we were paid by the network. Buddy and Chris, or maybe Chris and Buddy had to bring their own cameras, while we supplied the memory cards. I advanced one of them—whoever Cinni's ex boyfriend was—with enough money to rent a mini van for the day. One large enough to carry us and our equipment and the doubloons which were divided into 15 backpacks with a thousand doubloons with the same color in each pack. Lucy Laroux suggested that I hired, as a general contractor, Gene, a light skinned African American who I actually knew from when I lived in Caesar, Mississippi when I shared the Trailer with Glen. Gene had just gotten out of prison. He would drive the van and, while we were doing our thing, find some stooges to distribute the doubloons.

On the ride to New Orleans, I sat in the back—third—row of seats, not because I like riding in the back, but because Gene never stops talking. Lucy Laroux, who was apparently his parole officer too, apparently suggested I hire him so she wouldn't have to revoke his parole. She easily got dispensation so he could leave the state for the day. I had no idea if he was fucking her, munching her muffin, or just spying on us, or any combination of the three. But I knew he'd work cheap, if not always very effectively.

Shortly after we got on I-10, I told the kids that I didn't have anything scripted, that they should just try to have fun, or to look like they were having fun.

Then, Brittney asked: "Is it all right if I flash my tits?"

"Go for it," Billy said.

"No!" I exclaimed. "If you want to do that at school, or even on the school bus, as long as we're not recording it, I don't care. But not when we're tying to make a show. You and Lindsey are both too young to be flashing your breast on camera."

"I never had any intention of exposing myself," Lindsey said, upset that I would even suggest that she might.

"Only because you're even more flat chested than mom," Billy said. At this point, Lindsey punched Billy on the arm.

"Enough! Let's save the arguing for things we can actually put on our show."

"Want me to stop filming this?" Cinni's ex boyfriend

asked.

"No, not yet anyway. We might be able to salvage some of it. This is supposed to be a fun day with the happy Morgan kids. By the way, the Second Amendment Patriot channel changed its name to the Patriot God and Gun channel, not that it's a religious channel," I hoped not anyway. "But it would be a bad idea for even Cinni, who's 18 and legally allowed to be filmed topless, to be shown flashing her breast on a network that has 'God' it its name."

"I wasn't planning on flashing my tits either," Cinni said, unfortunately.

"Somethings are just in bad taste," Buddy or Chris said, the one who wasn't Cinni's old boyfriend. "No one would respect a girl who would expose herself like that."

"Amen!" both Cinni and Lindsey said.

I was almost certain Cinni bra size was a C cup, my favorite brassiere—and breast—size and would have loved to have seen her flash those bodacious tatas. But that wasn't the purpose of the trip and I wouldn't have thought of it if Brittney hadn't mentioned it. Brittney was possibly the smartest of the kids, though Anne and Glen were doing a pretty good job of dumbing her down. When I first met her she was quite inquisitive and it was obvious that she had a brain in her head, but in the next few months since then maybe when her breasts went from an A cup to a very disproportional, for an eleven year old, B cup, and possibly a C cup, she seemed to have lost at least 20 or 30 IQ points. (Admittedly, what I perceive as her IQ loss could be attributed to her ADHD medication or whatever he medication was for.) Although I wouldn't say that like some men think with their dicks, she thinks with her breasts, it's possible that their size has had a psychological effect on her, as they might on probably any eleven year old girl. During the same time, she gained a lot of weight, so she probably doesn't have many eleven, twelve, thirteen and fourteen year old boys hitting on her all the time.

Once we got to Nawleans, as tourist love to call it, and found a good spot to watch the parades, I gave Gene $300 to pay some people to distribute the doubloons. Gene would stay with the van. I asked Buddy or Chris to stay with him to film anything worthy of being added to the episode, which, in his opinion, were long takes of various street walkers, and even a few clips of women flashing their tits and one clip of an extremely well hung, inebriated man wearing an orange devil costume urinating on the sidewalk.

We mainly just recorded the parades and the assorted people running around in all kinds of costumes ranging from silly to trashy to outrageously flamboyant. Unfortunately, the kids behaved so I didn't get any good footage of them, unless Lindsey and Billy looking bored out their minds was usable.

We decided we had seen enough by around 6pm. I agreed to take them out to eat before we headed back. Brittney and Lindsey wanted to go to the Cafe Du Monde, but the line was a mile long. Cinni insisted that we go to a Crazy Burger, so we sat in a large family size booth and discussed the day. (Or course, the festivities were still going on, but it was getting late.) I was hoping they would ad lib something worth showing on the episode, but they mainly just complained about one thing or another. Billy complained that he didn't see any woman flash their tits.

"We did," Gene said. "We also saw a Chalmation in a devils costume with a 12 inch cock taking a piss. Buddy got it on camera."

"Thanks Gene," I said. "Please use less colorful language. We're trying to tape this."

"I also saw a transvestite, I mean a drag queen, being double teamed by two guys wearing pirate costumes in an alley. I don't think Buddy filmed it."

"What's double teamed?" Lindsey asked.

"It's when a girl or guy bends over--"

"Gene, enough!"

At this point I almost decided we should keep going. That this could make a bloopers or an outtakes DVD. But it was way too graphic for an adult to be telling it to an eleven or a couple of thirteen year old kids on cable.

"Can I explain?" Cinni asked.

"Go ahead," I said, trying to sound both disgusted, beaten and unable to stop the inevitable. Of course, I actually wanted to hear what she wanted to say.

"It's like when Billy bends over and gets fucked in the ass while he is also sucking a dick!"

# Chapter 10 Living with our Mistakes

I was taking what I like to call a creative nap, where I try to get inspiration from my dreams. This rarely worked, but I was looking for some way to piece together the Mardi Gras footage to make a decent episode. I must have been in REM sleep because I had a boner when loud pounding on my door woke me.

"Who—what is it?" I asked.

"It's me you bastard," Anne shouted. "We got to *talk*!"

I got up, put my flip flops on, and opened the door.

"Wha-"

"Did you tell Brittney she could flash her tits on the bus?"

"Hell, no," I said. "Why the fuck would I—" and then I remembered. "Well maybe, but I didn't think she would—"

"What sick kind of a bastard are you?"

"—or should do it. Definitely not. I was trying—"

"Tha's just fuckin' demendid!"

"—to explain that she shouldn't flash in New Orleans because—"

"You fuckin' pervert!"

This tirade went on for fifteen minutes with the upshot being that if Brittney got suspended or expelled from school then she and Glen would kick me out of the house.

Anne had me call the middle school and talk to the principal. I tried to explain what had happened, that it was all my fault, that I was a terrible role model for children, and that I jokingly told her that it would be better to flash her boobs in school or on the school bus than in the crowd at Mardi Gras. S/he asked me if Anne was making me say this and I replied yes, but it was basically true: that I didn't want her to flash in Nawleans and was misinterpreted. Apparently the school superintendent had already decided not to suspend or expel her. They were glad she wasn't fighting with the other students and felt that flashing, by no means permissible under any circumstances, was, in her case anyway, a step in the right direction. I talked for a few more minutes, mainly about what a bright kid I thought Brittney was but not really suited for home schooling and finally thanking the principal a few times.

I told Anne, taking complete credit for something that had already been decided, that I had talked them out of suspending her.

"Just be careful what you say around her," she said. "You know how impressible children her age are."

I wanted to say 'impressionable' but decided to quit while I was ahead. And she left my room under almost friendly terms.

I really wouldn't mind that much if I got kicked out of the house. The kids were usually noisy and disrespectful. Granny was a delusional, alcoholic, pot head, grifter. Anne was a sentimental—about her children anyway—control freak and Glen was catatonic most of the time, when he's not at work, playing with his pups or talking football anyway.

I had a cheap doorknob lock that anyone could open with a penknife. I was always worried the kids were going to steal my shit when I was away; or worse, catch me masturbating when I wasn't. I could just imagine Anne giving me a hard time about jerking off in front of the kids when I was doing it alone with my door locked. Some things I didn't need and getting caught chocking the chicken was one of my biggest fears.

More important than getting caught jerking off was my fear that my guitars might get stolen, especially my Telecaster Deluxe which I've had since the mid-nineties and used as my primary ax since I lost my Rickenbacker. I'd hate to lose my Strat or SG, but I have no real sentimental attachment for them. I never forgave myself for letting a serial killer steal my Rickenbacker, which was the last thing my mother gave me before she died when I was twelve.

Since they didn't want me messing with the woodwork of

my door, I compromised by getting a mail order gun safe. Although it was neither fire nor water resistant it was designed to be theft proof and could be screwed into the wall for added protection.

**I purchased the American Patriot God and Gun Safe model 24H, which was designed to keep Guns safe and in a special humidity controlled cabinet on the upper shelf to keep ammunition and even the Holy Bible dry. I'm sure this safe will bring me years of joy and I gladly endorse this product.** [ED NOTE: Is this a plug?  Very unprofessional!]

As an added bonus, I could keep my guns in there too, except for my pistol grip Mossberg Pump, which I kept under my pillow or between the mattress and headboard base. Getting a gun safe had been suggested by Laroux but I told her I didn't have enough money until I realized that in a larger one I could keep my guitars and the camera equipment relatively safe.

So far I've managed to get around from mentioning it too much, but the house is in a predominately black neighborhood and, although I don't want to perpetuate any negative stereotypes about African Americans, the family has had things stolen from their property including a lawnmower that I gave them when they first moved.

Anyway, Laroux thinks I got the gun safe to keep the guns away from Anne and the kids. The family thinks it's because "we" live in a mainly black neighborhood.  And although they are both partially true, the whole truth is a lot less complicated. My main fear is that Anne or the kids might steal my more expensive crap.  I worried a lot about my wallet with all my Cash, Credit and Debit Cards too.

Of course, I could be wrong about the kids and hope that I am.  Wrong about Anne too.  According to Glen, she went to prison for either making or distributing Meth, though she told Glen that it was her former boyfriend who was making or distributing it, and that she went to prison because she wouldn't testify against him. As much as I would like to say bullshit, I admit that it's possible. I even knew a few people who seemed to actually brag that their woman took the rap for the when she was caught with their junk, so it wasn't that hard to believe.

In order to finish the third episode, I decided to take the van back to Nawleans again, this time recording everything on Tuesday evening after school. I gave everyone flash cards with specific dialog often as an impetus for improvised answers. I asked Gene to please watch his language, that this was a prime time family show. Before starting, I said to everyone: "If you're going to ad lib the answers to the questions on the flash cards, please use language we can use on the show. If not, please stick to the script."

Once we started going, and the camera was running, Billy said: "I hope we see some bitches flashing their breast."

"They are called 'women' Billy," Cinni said, sticking to the answer script, at least as far as bitches went. "Bitches is a derogatory term demeaning to women."

"I'm sorry. But I do hope I see some women flashing their breasts!"

"Well you certainly won't see me flashing my breasts," Lindsey said.

"What breasts?"

At which point Lindsey hit Billy on the shoulder, still on script.

"Can I flashed my ti—breasts?" Brittney asked?

At this point Cinni said that flashing encouraged men to degrade women—followed by basically the same thing that Buddy or Chris said on Sunday about flashing and Lindsay said "amen" and Gene said "you got that right sister."

Then they started talking about transvestites and how they will all go to hell if they don't repent and that probably everyone who lives in Nawleans is almost certainly condemned to hell unless they find Jesus and move out of that sinful town. This sort of idiotic banter went on all the way to Nawleans and back. There wasn't very much substance to it. The Mardi Gras episode was by far the fluffiest one we made. And, ultimately, we decided to add an appendage about Brittney nearly being suspended from school for flashing her breasts in class and on the school bus, only instead of blaming me, we focused on her being influenced by the unholy activities she saw in New Orleans, not that she actually saw anyone flashing, but why let the truth get in the way of trying to salvage the episode. We ended the episode with Brittney saying a prayer and thanking God for keeping her out of trouble and then she promised to never flash again, or, at least, not until she goes away to Bible Camp in the summer.

# Chapter 11 Dinner with the Deacon

Our fourth episode was going to be about politics, and, although a lot of it would focus on the second amendment, Glen and Gene ended up taking a lot of abuse for being liberals. In reality, Glen was about as liberal as Rush Limbaugh would be while visiting the Dominican Republic. Glen was only liberal, in the fact that he was a neo-liberal libertarian and cared more for the rights of corporations and businesses and almost nothing as far as human rights are concerned when they aren't employers or Gun Owners. His only liberal beliefs were that drugs and prostitution should be legalized, beliefs many democrats don't really care about, especially legalizing prostitution. Back when we shared the trailer I used to joke with him that he wouldn't be happy until they abolished the minimum wage and his job was outsourced to India.

Although I would never admit it, I was probably more liberal than Glen on just about all issues except gun control. Not that I was ever a democrat or supported Obama or anything crazy like that. My worse liberal fault was that I was pro-choice, not that I'm pro-abortion except in cases where I thought I was the father. I was pro-life until I thought I had knocked up a woman in the mid-nineties. When I heard that she was pregnant, I instantly went from being pro-life to pro-choice and have been ever since, even after finding out that she was probably nearly two months pregnant when I balled her. In any case, she never tried hitting on me up for child support and apparently someone else tested positive on a DNA test. Of course, this isn't the sort of thing I talk about to anyone living in this house which has four illegitimate children living in it.

Along the same lines, since I moved to Mississippi, I haven't told anyone down here that I was one eighth Native American. I also wouldn't admit that I was glad that the North won the civil war. It's one thing to have values up north where they can make a difference. But down here we're living in a different time zone where the clocks are set back an hour and common sense set back to the twilight zone.

I decided I would hire Gene to pretend to be the liberal gun control freak. He was smart enough to hold out for a thousand dollars, but he wasn't going to get paid unless he was convincing. And for a thousand dollars, he had to be liberal about everything.

I figured we could have a Presidents day episode. I didn't let the fact that it was a few days after Presidents Day stop us. We needed some kind of gimmick so we could talk about politics and how evil, sinful and stupid liberals were and how they wanted to take away our guns so only criminals and the police, who are mainly agents of Obama, would be armed. I forbade any conversation about Obama being the Antichrist or a Muslim, insisting that we should save that for the Easter episode.

The Scene: Sunday Night Dinner—shot on Thursday—with Gene pretending to be a Deacon at Anne's church.

Lights, Camera, Bull Shit!

"How can anyone be against background checks? Do you really want to allow criminals and the mentally ill to have access to firearms?" Gene asked. Of course Gene was a criminal—or ex-con anyway—so he apparently knew what he was talking about.

"Maybe not criminals, and definitely not while they are still in prison," Glen said. "But forbidding the mentally ill from having a gun is as prejudiced as not letting a black person drink from the same water fountain as a white person or not allowing a blind person to drive. It's discrimination pure and simple and as a country, we should have out grown these restrictions to our human rights."

"Amen," said simultaneously by both Anne and Cinni.

Gene, who has seen real discrimination in his life probably

couldn't believe what he was hearing.

"There's really no comparison," Gene said.

"You may hate African Americans Gene," Lindsay said, "But we believe they should have the same rights we do, same with the mentally ill and the blind."

"I'm the only one here who's black!"

"And you shouldn't hate yourself for it," Anne said. Then she ad libbed: "I have good news for you Gene. God still loves you even though you are black. Just take Jesus in your heart and He'll forgive you for being—for everything that's wrong with you."

At this point it was obvious that Gene was thinking about getting a gun and shooting at least two people, Anne and Glen, probably also Lindsey and me and maybe a couple of the other kids. . .

But he stayed in character and mentioned all the gun deaths, deliberate and accident.

At this point Billy ad libbed and blamed the gun deaths on evolution and how could liberals "believe in evolution and be against the one thing that comes close to proving survival of the fittest and the natural selection of those who have the biggest and best guns." Not sure anyone understood the point Billy was trying to make. I wasn't sure if he was trying to talk about assault rifles, artillery or penis size. I had asked them all *not* to discuss evolution and global warming figuring these were issues we could devote whole episodes to both subjects and blame global warming on gay marriage. I was hoping no one would ask Billy to elucidate what he was trying to say, and bring the discussion back to guns without using the e-word. In any case, it was better to talk about evolution than climate change.

"Next you'll be blaming guns for causing global warming?" Brittney asked, directing her question to Gene.

"No, I blame cow farts and carbon emissions for global

warming," Gene said.

"Blaming cows!" Billy said. "Now that's funny."

I don't think Gene was going to become a vegan anytime soon, but even I knew cow flatulence was climate change enemy number two, no pun intended, or possibly three or four.

"*They* do try to blame cow farts for global heating," Glen said. "It's one of their main arguments for why people should become vegans, or, at the very least, vegetarians.   Not that there's any truth in it."

"All flatulence contains methane, an inflammable carbon based gas," Gene said and then asked: "Can I get seconds on the pot roast please?"

"The only way I would ever become a vegetarian," Glen ad libbed, while passing the serving plate with pot roast to Gene, "is if the only choice I had was between being a vegetarian and being a cannibal."

At this point Billy burps and says: "Excuse me!"

Brittney changed the subject completely by asking, off script, why it was against the law for her to have sex with Cinni's boyfriends.

"Brittney," Anne commanded,"you're way to young to be having sex!"

"All the other girls in my class are doing it.  But the boys in class won't fuck me.  They say I'm too fat."

"The age of consent is set high for a reason," Gene said. "The younger you are the more likely you are to make stupid decisions.   Decisions that can effect your whole life in a negative way.  Many men will try to take advantage of you and tell you all kinds of lies to get in your—well, to have their way with you."

"Boys will lie too," Billy said, "but they're not as good liars."

"This is not a proper discussion," Anne said, who, to her credit, waited until she was sixteen before having her first child, or giving birth anyway.

"It's something that both liberals and conservatives can agree on, right Glen?" Gene said.

Glen gave a somewhat unorthodox libertarian answer that children should have the right to both work and have control of their bodies, but that maybe, bearing in mind that he hated creating new laws, that kids should have to pass a consent awareness test before they could have sex or prostitute themselves. Not, he add, that he was *not* in favor of child or even teen prostitution, just that they should have the right to work same as adults.

"Is that the official NAMBLA, I mean Libertarian position?" Gene asked.

"Don't bring Nambla into this," Granny said. "They might want to make Billy their 2015 poster boy."

"What's nambla?" Lindsey asked.

"The North American Marlon Brando Lookalike Association," Billy said, quoting a *South Park* character. "And I don't look anything like Marlon Brando, even when he was young."

"They advocate pedophilia and pederasty," Gene said.

"That ain't Marlon Brando you idiots," Granny said. "That's that Man Boy Gay Love group. An' don' mock Marlon Brando. He used to be da bomb. I'd let him shag me anytime. I'd fuck him six ways to Sunday and I'd gladly go to hell for it!"

"Gram, damn it," Anne said, "please watch your language. Some of us are trying to eat here."

"Just sayin' Brando was hot, maybe not by the time he made the Godfather, but the young Brando I'd do in the confessional at a christening' even if one of us had to hold the baby."

"Gram," Anne asked, possibly trying to change the subject, "when did you ever go to a confessional?"

"I blew a seminary student in—"

"Forget I asked!"

"So who was the boy Brando loved?" Lindsey asked.

"I don't think Brando went that way," Gene said while Granny almost simultaneously said "Damn right he didn't!"

"On *South Park* a Brando look alike liked Eric Cartman," Billy said, though not really in the same way as the other Nambla people did."

"Stop the Brando bashing you bastards!" Granny exclaimed. "The only gay thing he ever did was, in his best picture, *The Wild One*, instead of riding a Harley like a real man, he rode a Triumph. But maybe he wasn't a big enough star at the time to demand the best. Tha' don' mean he took it up the ass or anythin' like tha' you sick bastards!"

And with that, Granny got up and left for her trailer.

Gene, now on a soapbox, said: "The nambla I mentioned had nothing to do with Marlon Brando, but rather the MB stands for Man Boy and the LA for Love Association and not just Liberals and conservatives are against it, so is nearly every Gay and Lesbian group in the country." Which was almost certainly true, but I doubt if any of them actually believed that nor would their target audience.

"One of the reasons we need the second amendment is so families can protect their children from these pervs." Anne said.

"That's why there are laws!" Gene said. "If they get caught they go to jail and there they often end up doing the hardest time possible!"

"Laws won't help Billy after he's been fucked in the ass and turned into a swish," Anne said. At times she apparently believed it had actually happened and that he really was gay.

"Not that it wouldn't be detrimental to Billy if he was sodomized, but it would be the damage to his psyche that would be the real problem."

"Fuck his delicate psyche, I don't want a fuckin' homo in the family!"

"What if he just goes homo for just one episode," Lindsey said, forgetting we were not to discuss programming while recording. "Then we could send him to a Jesus Pray the Gay Away camp to get cured and then in the next episode, or the end of this one, we find that he actually had sex with a slut who just looked like a guy and that we all came to the wrong conclusion."

"She'd have to be pretty," Billy said. "I don't want to fuck a dog on tv!"

"No one's getting fucked on TV," Anne said. "I'll allow a blowjob, but you have to wear a condom."

"Ah come on! Condoms are sinful mom!" Billy said.

"It wouldn't be used to prevent pregnancy, you stupid idiot, but disease."

"You could just have the young lady tested first," Gene said, dropping his liberal affectation. "No guy wants to wear a jimmy hat when getting his dick sucked," he paused, and then said: "Actually, since you wouldn't be able to show it, why not just hire an actress and simulate the whole thing. No need for any actual contact at all."

"Damn!" Billy said. "That ain't no fun at all. I want to at least jizz on her face."

"That's gross Billy!" said Cinni or Lindsey.

"Ah, gross Billy!" said Lindsey or Cinni, simultaneously with the preceding comment.

"It's not like our programs are scripted or planned out in advance," Glen said.

"They aren't?" Anne said. " You could o' fooled me."

At this point I said: "*Cut!* Remember, this is supposed to be a reality TV show, not a sitcom. So when Glen or anyone else says something like that, agree with him. Otherwise we can't use it. As it is, we'll have to rewrite a lot of what was said tonight.   But we got a lot of good stuff, things we can use in two or three episodes.   And remember, we have to bleep all swear words.

"Also," I went on, "it would probably alienate our projected audience if a regular member of the cast was gay, even for one episode.   Not that it's all that uncommon, but usually, in the deep south anyway, they have the good sense to stay in the closet."

"We don' have any fags in our family," Anne said.   "This is not New Jersey.   No one in this family ever got gay married or ever will, and that includes you Mister!"   These last five words were addressed to Billy.

I told them it was time to discuss Obamacare and went back to my video recorder.

Lindsey asked: "Which is worse?   Granny being a drunk or Granny possibly being a liberal?"

"Liberal is much worse Hon," Anne said.   "A drunk can always find God and get straight like me and Glen.   But liberals are just evil."

"The worst thing about liberals is they never did anything for this country but make it worse," Glen said.

"Every social advancement was caused by Liberals from unions, social security, workplace and environmental protections and, most recently the Affordable Care Act," Gene said.

"Bullshit!" Anne said.   "They are all commie tools to destroy America and Obamacare is worst than slavery.   I heard that on Fox News and it was said by the smartest colored fellow who ever lived."

"Affordable health should be a right, not a privileged of the prosperous."

"I heard obamacare was worse then the Holocaust," Brittney said.

"You're damn right it is." Anne said.   "Obamacare is the

worst thing to happen to America since the jews killed Jesus. God only knows how many people are going to die because of it."

"You people are crazy," Gene said.

"You just like it cause Obama added reparations to coloreds in Obamacare so that you nig-, you bla-, you African Americans get to go to the front of the line when receiving health care and that you can sell your front row health passes to rich people."

"It's designed to keep health care cost low and heath insurance affordable."

"It's designed so hospitals have to close down and doctors go broke. The only thing worse than Obamacare in the world today is the gays trying to redefine marriage!"

"Marriage gets redefined as meaningless every time someone who is married gets a divorce."

"Next thing you'll want to allow Billy to marry Dallas."

"Dallas does not have the mental capacity to legally commit to marriage."

At this point, Brittney left the table, picked up Dallas and put him on the table saying: "Dallas is as smart as any liberal who ever lived."

And being a smart chihuahua, Dallas knocks over several glasses before he gets to the serving plate with a few remaining slices of pot roast on it and nearly chokes on one of the larger slices. At this point Glen starts slicing small pieces of it for Dallas.

"I guess he's smarter than libertarians too," Gene added, getting the last word in. . .

I had to admit that the conversation was over the top preposterous, even though I scripted a good part of it, but I was hoping our target audience would believe it. Of course, many of the ideas were recycled from Fox News, which is even more honest than I am, if that's possible! I made up the part about reparations figuring it's probably written into Obamacare, but no one has noticed it yet.  Gene was doing much better than expected and only broke character once.  He also managed to keep his language relatively clean.  He came up with a good reply to Anne's Gay Marriage comparison though it might have kept her for going on a triage against Gay Marriage.  I was just thinking of adding him as a regular when he said:

"If Billy gets the bug from being ass fucked you'll be glad you got Obama-care."

"If Billy goes gay he's out of here.  He doesn't even have to get aids.  I won't have any gays in this family.  You hear me?"

"I'm not gay," Billy cried!  "I may not have had a lot of girlfriends, but I would never be with a guy!"

"Cinni said Billy had two girlfriends," Brittney said.  "She called them his left and his right.  But I've never seen him with them."

"They sneak under his sheets at night," Cinni said.

"They just better not be a guys lefts and rights, tha's all I can say," Anne said, which may have been the dumbest thing said this evening, but hopefully still good for ratings.

"When I'm famous I'll be banging five or six bitches a day.  Then you'll be sorry for all the crap you been saying about me."

"Billy," Gene said, trying to sound compassionate, but coming across as condescending "it sounds like you're trying to over compensate for the feelings you have about men.  You don't have to be ashamed for how you feel."

"That's true Billy," Glen said.  "But just remember that a dick sucked can't be unsucked.  So if you haven't started doing those things, don't start now.  Someday you'll find a girl who will love you for who you are, not who you pretend to be."

"Billy with a girlfriend.  Now that's funny!" Lindsey said.

"Billy, just have faith in God," Anne said.  "If He can walk on water and then turn it into wine, then He can find you a girl dumb enough to be your soul mate."

"I heard Billy did something really queer with a girl named JJ the other day," Brittney said.

"All I did was lick a girl's privates for a few minutes. I don't see why that makes me queer."

"What girl?" Anne asked, sounding angry.

"Jannie Johns who lives across the street. She's in my English class."

"A colored girl?"

Billy nodded.

"All right Billy!" Glen said, raising his hand, palm open. "High five!"

And Billy slapped Glens hand.

"Billy, you shouldn't be messing with black girls," Anne said. "You have no idea what you might catch!"

"She's a nice girl mom," Billy said. "When we're both sixteen I'm going to marry her." I found out later that none of this was true. Billy had nearly kissed her once, but he didn't because he was scared his mom would find out and beat the crap out of him. By this point though, he was sick of being called queer, so he figured, hoped actually, that this would change the focus of their verbal attacks on him, which it did.

"Nice girl my ass! I'm sure she's the one who stole Little Arthur." *Little Arthur* was the name of the push lawn mower I gave Glen after he moved out of the trailer we were sharing in Caesar."

"Why would she want a lawn mower?"

"To sell, stupid, so she can buy some crack! Stay away from her!"

"Billy listen to your mother," Gene, of all people, said breaking character again. "Unless you got a ten or eleven inch pecker, you'll never be able to satisfy a black woman."

"I love her enough to cut an inch or two off if necessary," Billy said. Fortunately, everyone knew that was bullshit. But it seemed like good time to pull the plug, so to speak.

"OK, CUT!" I said. "Thanks everyone. That was some good stuff tonight. You were a bit rough on Billy, but he took it like a man and came out of his corner swinging in the final rounds with a few really good lines. One, I think, almost straight out of the original version of *Deep Throat*."

"Billy," Anne said. "I don't want you watching porn."

"I'm sure he heard the phrase somewhere else," I said. "Or maybe he made it up or really has a 12 inch penis."

No one was interested in pursuing the subject of Billy's penis size which left him a little dignity. I told him we'd lay off the gay stuff, but that he should try to stay on good terms with the girl across the street just in case his mom starts harassing him again. According to Glen, all the men in Anne's life were complete bastards and I guess she thinks that men who aren't complete bastards are in some way defective—Glen being the exception, of course. Since Billy wasn't a complete bastard— bear in mind that he was only thirteen and there was still plenty of time for him to pick up bad habits—she probably felt that there is something wrong with him and that, obviously, he was maybe a little gay which seems to be her worst fear concerning her children. The thought that he might be another exception hasn't occurred to her, at least not yet. Growing up in a house with nothing but women, he might have picked up a few feminine traits like looking at his fingernails or the bottom of his shoes/feet in the "wrong way." I decided that I'd try to set her fear at ease by suggesting that maybe he's a future serial killer or something even worse like a potential liberal, or on an even faster train to hell, a future liberal politician.

I told Gene I'd try to write him into most episodes as our token liberal. At this point, we could only pay him two thousand per episode, the same as Laroux and Granny, but I'd try to come up with a little more since he also worked as a stage hand. In the mean time, he should study enough liberal politics to be conversant on some seditious liberal topics. He should especially read up on evolution and global heating, so he would seem to have a good grasp on these issues. Although these were briefly mentioned, I would try to save most of the climate change discussion for another episode. I would discard Billy's comments about guns proving evolution, since it really didn't make any sense and no one followed up on it. We would still devote a whole show on evolution, maybe with Gene using Walmart shoppers as examples of evolution in progress, though possibly not this season. I didn't want to have too many episodes where they just sat around talking. More action was needed—more walk, less talk. . .

Before Anne went to sleep, I recorded her asking God to ". . . please keep Billy from becoming gay and also keep him away from black girls. Maybe he could find a cute retarded girl who will like him in spite of him being himself!"

I spent the next day editing the fourth episode and had it satisfactory completed by the end of the afternoon. I wasn't happy with the third episode but I thought the second and fourth were great. Since there was plenty left over from the fourth episode, I decided to add some of the dialog to various parts of the third episode. But if the pilot was a B+ and the second and fourth episodes both As, the third was either a D- or an F.

I decided I should have a discussion with Anne about Billy. The next time I saw her when no one else was around I said:

"Billy's at an age when kids often experiment sexually. Usually, if they do happen to have one or two gay experiences, they get disgusted with what they did and never do it again. It doesn't mean they are gay, just trying to find themselves. No matter what though, it is vitally important that they know they have a loving family."

"Billy knows we love him and we will continue to as long as he doesn't run around chasing after guys."

"I'm sure Billy doesn't. But if he does, he'll need

unconditional love."

"If he does, he can get unconditional love from his gay lovers."

"He really needs it from his family," I said. "He's less likely to do something really stupid if he knows he's loved at home."

"As long as he stays away from guys and black girls he will be."

"But wouldn't you rather have him date a black girl than a man?"

"He's too young to be dating anyone. He's only been to a couple school dances and none of the girls would dance with him. Maybe they intuitively knew he was queer."

"They probably just thought he was a geek, in other words someone who was smarter rather than muscular. Has good grades rather than good looks."

"Billy's very han'some."

"The important thing is that he survives adolescences, not always an easy thing."

"He survived foster homes."

This went on and on without getting anywhere. I eventually got her to concede, not that I was trying to, that it was better for him to date black girls that it was for him to be sucking dick. But she didn't want him to get married until after he went to college. She didn't want him to marry a black girl, period, but realized that once he was an adult, she couldn't stop him. She just wouldn't go to the wedding. At least she didn't ask to meet the girl.

I found out later that Anne feared that Billy had gotten molested while he was in a foster home while she was in prison. Most people would have been a lot more worried about their daughters, but apparently Anne took if for granted that the girls would get messed with either by the older children living there or the adults running the homes. I never heard any of the kids talk about being molested and felt Anne's fears were groundless. She knew there was nothing she could do about it if they had been molested and would only feel guilty for either getting caught, or being in a relationship with the wrong guy, or both, which caused the state child welfare department to take charge of the children while she was in custody.

They had a chance now to change the course of their lives for the better. If things went right, they'd have nearly forty thousand dollars per child, before taxes anyway, to invest in their college education and a lot more flowing in if there were additional seasons of *The Morgan Family Rules!!!*

# Chapter 12 Cinni's Roux Gospel

I decided the next episode would be where the kids try to form a Christian Rock Band, assuming one of them could sing. As it turned out, all four could sing well enough to be considered to be singing in the right key, though all but Lindsey needed Auto Tune. I figured we could have four episodes giving each kid a chance to show what they can do in their own episode.

None of them were musicians, but Cinni could play chords and simple melodies on a Casio Keyboard, Billy knew around 10 basic chords on the guitar and both Lindsey and Brittney played recorders, though Brittney only in the lower register. Glen and me could both play guitar, and we'd bring Mark in to play bass. I'd check with Gene to see if he could play drums, but, if not, we could always use a drum machine, or the rhythm patterns on Cinni's Casio. Hell, we weren't really aspiring to rise above the level of crude.

I loaned Glen fifty dollars so he could get his guitar out if hock so I wouldn't have to let him use my Strat or SG. He was not even allowed to look at my Telecaster.

At this point, my worse nightmare came true. After finding out Gene couldn't play drums, I decided to eventually get a drum machine, but, for the time being, to use Cinni's Casio, which had a couple hundred rhythm patterns. Unfortunately, Gene mentioned to Laroux that we were looking for a drummer for at least four episodes. Instead of finding us another ex-con to add to our expanding cast of regulars, she said that she played snare drums in High School and bass drum while at college and still had both drums in addition to a pair of floor tom toms and managed to coerce a position as backing band drummer on at least four episodes. When I said we really didn't have any additional money—not even enough for a drum machine—she said she was happy with her AP shares and the only concession she wanted from us was for us to allow her to submit some songs she wrote to the kids to see if any of them would want to sing them.   She would also renounce all broadcast royalties involving our show.   It didn't surprise me that she was an aspiring song writer, but she couldn't believe any of us would be interested in the crap she was shitting out, but. . .

As it turned out, Cinni really liked the following Laroux Composition:

With a pill bottle in my hand
No one can understand
And though broken I'd still bend
Going nowhere with no end.

At the lowest point I found
Going up was hell ward bound.
All I owned was sorrow
Past passing into tomorrow.

And now I yield for no one
Only Jesus
Knows the degradation I was going through
And now I know there's no one
Only Jesus
Who can deliver me to where I'm going to.

I wasn't going anywhere
Lost between here and there
So sinful I didn't care
Not knowing You were near
I gave up and giving in
I heard a knock sounding within
And at the end I found the start
With JC knocking at my heart.

And now I feel for no one
Only Jesus
Knows the situation I was living in
And now I know there's no one
Only Jesus
Who can deliver me from my lowly life of sin.

I wasn't going anywhere
The morning sun was just a glare
I was blinded by a haze
And was lost inside a maze.

You brought me to my knees
Then You listened to my pleas
And filled my heart with grace
As Your love glows on my face

And now I kneel for no one
Only Jesus
Knows the degradation I was going through
And now I know there's no one
Only Jesus
Who can deliver us to where we're going to.

And now I kneel for no one
Only Jesus
Knows the situation I was living in.
And now I know there's no one
Only Jesus
Who can wash me clean of that sick life of sin.

The song had a really easy A, E7, F#m, D chord
progression probably more appropriate for pop music than

Christian, but it seemed to work.  Cinni asked Lucy Laroux to make the following changes: To change the verse structure from 12 bars to 16 bars with the first eight bars of the first verse having her doing keyboard solo, and in the second verse, during the first eight bars, a guitar solo by Billy, or, at least, guitar synced by Billy.  They both played before the third verse and finally, between the third and fourth revised chorus, Cinni wanted Brittney and Lindsey to play dueling recorder solos, at times alternating, at other times, playing together, for 16 bars.

When it came to actually recording it, Cinni sang all the vocals, except, during the chorus, when Brittney, Lindsey and Billy sand backing vocals, but only during the "Only Jesus" parts.  Instrumentally, their playing sucked, and I ended up playing all the solos including both tracks of final two recorder solos.

I'm not particularly proud of the convincing it took to get me to play all the non-percussion instrumental solos on the song.  Lets just say that maybe Lucy Laroux only gets on her knees for Jesus, but that Liz Roux got on her knees just to get a relatively competent musician to play on her song and make sure the final product was nicely polished.  And, of course, she wasn't exactly praying.  Or begging either.  This was actually a lot sicker than our previous encounters because we were at a fast food restaurant at the time and she followed me into the men's room.

Then again, the SOB in me enjoyed every minute of it, not that it lasted all that long.  I wouldn't have felt bad about it if I hadn't thought that she written the song at a low point in her life.  Perhaps she was even sincere and it was about a real religious awakening.  But, since she was now trying to commercially profit from it, fuck it, or, rather, in this case anyway, suck it.

Rather than blowing me, the stupid bitch actually offered me a fifty percent songwriting credit instead.  But when I turned her down, she seemed rather please that I preferred relinquishing all rights to the song, saying she felt obligated to offer. Ordinarily, session musicians *never* receive songwriting credits for improvising parts and solos and I can write my own crap and I don't need any credit from hers. . .

Part of me wanted to believe that the B&D games that Lucy was playing with me were over, but I was far from sure of that. And the fact that she was now in the backup band, made me regret the whole idea. Other then a few Kansas and Skillet songs, I was never a fan of Christian Rock. "Sympathy for the Devil" was the kind of music I liked. But Christian Rock was better than the country music that I imagined most of our shows projected viewers liked. I probably hated country music, at least the modern shit, more than our projected audience hated rap music.

The Cinni Gospel Rock singer episode was going to almost write itself. She had insisted on calling it "Gospel Rock" rather than "Christian Rock" for reasons she refused to articulate. We would start with 'Liz,' the backup group drummer, wearing a red wig to, she hoped, disguise herself, presenting her the song, and then Cinni asking for some changes in the instrumental solos. And then just follow the song through the creation process, only showing the kids playing their parts (without, of course, showing the editing process of adding my solos afterwards).

I would use the same approach with Brittney, Lindsey and Billy. Only in Billy's case I really wanted to heighten up the tension by trying to get him to wear a really tight Crop Top shirt and Hot Pants, figuring that would really send Anne over the edge. Don't get me wrong, I'd love it if the oldest daughter would wear hot pants and maybe a black bra, but I was pretty sure she wouldn't go for it. The middle daughter was too uptight and insecure about her body and the youngest daughter too fat in addition to being much too young. From what I knew of our channel, it could not get away with the kind of child exploitation, knowing only of one family channel that could get away with it.   Plus, since she had only very recently turned eleven, it would be somewhat inappropriate, even in rural white trash—well suburban white trash actually—Mississippi.

# Chapter 13 Brittney and Anne Duet

I asked Brittney if she wanted to sing in the next episode but it was at this point that Anne butted in saying she wanted to sing alongside her, maybe taking turns on the lines in the verse with both singing the chorus. I wouldn't say Anne leaned on Brittney, but I would say even a blind person would know that Brittney could never, at this stage of her life, turn her mother's request down. I have no idea who thought it up, though Anne claims she did, and she got Laroux to write her a chorus. I have no idea if this was ever done before, but they sang the Lord's Prayer acapella, then sang the chorus over and over again.

Brittney: Our Father
Anne: Who art in Heaven
Anne, Brittney: Hollowed be they Name
Brittney: Thy kingdom come
Anne: Thy will be done
Anne, Brittney: On earth as it is in Heaven
Brittney: Give us this day
Anne: Our daily bread
Anne, Brittney: And forgive us our trespasses
As we, forgive those, who trespass against us
Brittney: And lead us not into Temptation
Anne: But deliver us from Evil
Anne, Brittney: For thine is the kingdom and yeah, thine is the kingdom
Anne, spoken fast: Say it again
Anne, Brittney: For thine is the kingdom, the Power and the Glorrrrrrrryyyyy

Chorus
Amazing Graceland melody
I hear the Lord calling me.

Opening my eyes so I could see
My life was just a travesty.
Amazing Graceland destiny
But now I see that I am free
To escape from this comedy
Blessed in the Lord's reality

Repeat Chorus several times, with feeling.

For the songwriting credits they listed Jesus, L Roux, Yoko,
I mean A Morgan-Carter, B Morgan, G Carter.  They never
told me how they were going to pay Jesus his royalties and I
didn't ask.   The best thing about this song was I didn't
contribute to it at all.  Glen played all the guitar parts on the
chorus and Cinni did a competent job using her Casio to get the
bass parts.  I had offered to play the bass, but was glad Cinni
did instead.

The actual video recording was harder than usual because
there was obvious tension between Brittney and Anne, and, as
creepy as I am, I wasn't going to capitalize on it.  Instead, I got
a few shots illuminating the differences in bust sizes between
thirty-four year old Anne's A Cup, and, eleven year old
Brittney's way out of proportion B or C cup.  Part of me wanted
to give Brittney some effedren for a few weeks before videoing
it, to slim her down, but I was worried about the negative
effects it might have on her.  Considering her mother was an
addict and her grandmother an alcoholic and a pot head, I
figured Brittney could consider herself lucky if her worse
problem was an eating disorder.

We managed to avoid the in-fighting in these last two
episodes that we had in my of the earlier ones, so I decided to
shoot the seventh and the eighth shortly afterwards.  We'd
decide later which to use for a season finale.  Both Lindsey and
Billy were moody in their own way and they were often self-
conscious and sometimes even full of anger, which, under the

right circumstances, can set all kinds of sparks flying and cause all kinds of silly, irrational behavior.   It would probably be easier to get Lindsey to act tough like a dyke in a Christian Punk Rock group than to get Billy to dance around in hot pants, but both will create friction with their mother and, if nothing else, thirteen was a good age for kids to start rebelling against their parents, or, in this case, against their mother.  We just had to make sure that the kids didn't drive Anne back to using crack or crystal meth or whatever if was she was addicted to—the reports varied.

Instead of a Christian Rock or Gospel song, Lindsey wanted to sing Alanis Morissette's "Forgiven."  I had to listen to it a few times before I got it.  A nice, though not at all a rocking, rebellion song against religion.   Anne, who I believe liked Alanis Morissette, even referring to her as a poet I think, will probably snap at the list line of the song: *"You know how us Catholic girls can be"* if only to say something along the lines of "You ain't Catholic, you're Christian!   Everyone in the family is a Christian!"

Of course, I wasn't going to write Lindsey's lines for her and I had no idea how she really felt about religion or God or anything like that.  In spite of the whole family being Christian, I don't think any of them go to church on Sundays or even belong to a church.  Glen is probably more religious than any of them and I couldn't imagine him going to church when he had the chance to sleep late instead.  But I imagine all the kids were baptized, full immersion Baptist style.   And they all seemed to talk the talk, even Billy usually.

Rather than actually taking the time to learn the song and play four or five instrumental parts, I recorded a Karaoke version of "Forgiven" that was on YouTube.  We could always punk up the song later.  Lindsey didn't have the vocal range that Morissette had nor was she able to put the same emotion into the song, so that it sounded more like a superficial pop cover with none of the angst that was so popular in the nineties. Still, the vocals were clear and in key—clear enough so that the listener could actually understand the lyrics anyway.

What was really cool is she wanted to wear a lot of black make up in a goth, or emo, style and wear a tight back dorm shirt which would show more thigh than even I was comfortable with. She also wanted to die her hair black, but knew her mom wouldn't go along with it. Anne didn't have a problem with the short 'skirt' because it was so hot in the summer that everyone wore short shorts or short skirts, etc. The fact that we were recording this in March didn't have any effect on her philosophy.

"There's so many other better and more religious songs out there."

"But this one's cool and hasn't been done a thousand times."

"I like the slut look mom," Billy said. "I hate to say it, but it makes her look hot!"

"I'm supposed to look dark, you foo—"

"Billy, you shouldn't be thinking about your sister that way! It's perverted!"

"You fool," Lindsey continued, after her mother interrupted her, "maybe a little lost."

"I was just trying to complement her."

"Then don't call your sister a slut."

"I didn't. I said 'slut look' which is what everyone in school calls it. I wasn't bashing her for being a slut, or trying to shame her, just that I liked the look. Fuck, I'll never complement you again." He went in his room and slammed the door.

After a few minutes of superficial discourse, Lindsey said:

"I hope he's not beating off to me."

"The little perv betta not be!" Anne walked up to Billy's door, was about to knock or, more likely, pound on it. Decided to just open it and went in.

"Hey!"

"Billy, what the fuck you reading.  Is that some kind of sick porn?"

"It's science fiction.  It's for my English class."

"There's a little boy on the cover," Anne sounded really disgusted.  "Gay child porn, that's really gross."

"It's not porn.  It's about a military school in the future where all the students are geniuses.  I have to read it and write a report about it.  Talk it up with the teacher and the PTA and the School Board if you think it's porn."

"Well I just might young man and I will if I catch you beating off to it."

I texted Billy asking *what's the authors name?*

He texted back *Os card.*

*Enders game?*

*Y*

As much as I hated to interrupt, I felt obliged to tell Anne: "Orson Scott Card is known for being anti gay especially being against gay marriage and is, in many ways, ultra conservative. His biggest selling book, *Ender's Game*, isn't in any sexual way, pornographic.  It does have some violence in it, but no homosexuality.  Unless you actually catch him masturbating to the book, I don't think you have anything to worry about."

"I wasn't jerking off!"

"You better not be.  No one jerks off in this house!"

I was pretty sure just about everyone in the house masturbated, I certainly did.  And if Billy didn't yet, he probably would be soon.

Anne let Billy get back to his book, though I wasn't sure if she believed me about the author, who I had thought had written some brilliant stuff and had been reading since I was Billy's age, maybe younger.   But there was nothing pornographic about his writings.  I was telling the truth there. Otherwise, I would have let the argument continue.  Maybe I would give Billy some dirty books just to get Anne going.  Not porn, but maybe a little too graphic like Norman Spinrad's *Bug Jack Barron*. Samuel R. Delaney's *Dhalgren* would have been even better with its bisexual main character and its large cast of minorities, but I couldn't imagine him reading all eight hundred plus pages of it without being a real Science Fiction geek.

Actually, I thought it was a positive that the teacher would let the kids read something as readable as Ender's Game.   I think I had to read *Lord of the Flies* at around the same age, which was nowhere near as entertaining.   And some stuff they tried to get us to read was downright torture.

At this point I decided to invent a couple of secret admirers for Billy.   Maybe one was one of the girls in his English class. I'd have 'her' send him some SF books and later some dirty magazines.   Then I'd get the other one to send him a shemale magazine, something to really get Anne pissed.

But my most immediate goal was to get Billy to wear hot pants and a crop top for his song performance.   Of course crop tops on men were a stupid look in the eighties and even stupider looking now, but I could see it causing so much tension between Anne and Billy to actually get him kicked out of the house, which would be a great season finale.

I'd love to be able to script fights between Anne and the children or the children fighting among themselves like I did with political discussions, but none of them were good enough actors.   There was also always the chance one of them would go too far.   We didn't want to have anyone hitting anyone or Anne's parole getting revoked.   We especially didn't want Anne to actually hurt Billy and she might even be crazy enough to think she could save his immortal Soul by killing him before he goes completely gay.   Of course, being on parole is probably enough of an incentive to keep her from killing anyone.

I'll probably use the approach that if Billy can get over his rapping stage in no time at all, then he can outgrow his gay stage too.   And since he wasn't actually gay in the first place, it should be relatively easy to patch things up once the episode is finished.  But I'd have to get Billy to play along first, and at his age, that would be damn near impossible.  Probably my biggest failure while shooting the first season was not being able to get Billy to put on any kind of gay affectation or act.  He'd play a wigga rapper, but that was apparently the boundary he set for himself.

# Chapter 14 Hell is for Twins

Lindsey and Billy approached me about doing a couple songs together. Without saying it, I was sure they were worried that their mother might want to do a duet with them as she did with Brittney. Lindsey said she wanted to do Halestorm's *Hell is for Children*, perhaps tying to send a message with that choice of song. That, though, was just an inference on my part. Billy wanted to do a couple of real oldies. For the song to sing with Lindsey, he wanted to do Kansas' *Carry on my Wayward Son*, which would work in the Christian Rock vain of songs we were doing. He also wanted to do Jethro Tull's *Hymn 43* which was both a solid rocker and a condemnation of religious hypocrisy. In my opinion, we hit the jackpot with the second song he wanted to do. We would do them one at a time, after Anne had gone to work. I was pretty sure she'd hate the Tull song, think the Kansas song was about Billy homosexuality—which I was pretty sure was all in her head—and possibly think they were talking about her in the Pat Benitar/Halestorm song.

I had a perfect brainstorm, with the Hell is for Children song and asked them if they would do it costumed as young teen prostitutes, in Billy's case, of course, a male prostitute, though I would lead him to believe that his character's clients would be women. At the beginning, before the music starts, have Gene dressed as a stereotypical pimp, without actually laying a hand on them, telling them to get out and hit the streets. They seemed apprehensive about it, but I told Lindsey she could use the same outfit she wore when we videoed "Forgiven." Billy would just need some tight shorts, and maybe roll up your shirt to show as much skin as possible. At different parts in the video, the camera would shake a little and a bruise would appear on either Lindsey or Billy. By the end of the video they would be wearing bandages around their heads and maybe at least one cast. I told them that if they could pull this off, that they might both win an Emmy Award or an MTV

Video Award. Billy refused to wear tight shorts, though he would wear jeans and half way through the song, he's go shirtless, to show off his bruises.

Billy said "Carry On" would be done pretty much like Kansas did it, but for *Hymn 43*, Billy wanted a more electronic feel to it, especially on the guitar part of the Guitar/Bass hook, which would be done with a synthesizer effect or voice instead of a guitar.

"Or in addition to the guitar?" I asked without getting a positive response.

I didn't like it, but it would be original. The song would probably turn off a lot of the audience, but this was, after all, only a phase he was going through. I had visions of Billy, and now Lindsey, going through a lot of phases and, of course, a lot of growing pains. To a large extent, they would both play along with a lot of my BS, but they had their limits, damn it!

Anne didn't like being left out and being upstaged by the kids and got Glen into it and the two wanted to do a duet rendition of "Knocking on Heaven's Door," using Bob Dylan's original arrangement. I told them to go ahead, but I thought the whole family should do it, maybe with a different kid asking mom to take the badge, guns, crutch and disease or some such crap away from them. I suggested one of the kids sing the first line, Anne or Glen sing the second line, Glen or Anne sing the third line, both or all three the fourth line and everyone chip in of the chorus. As idiotic as this vocal arrangement was, they actually went along with it.

I thought the Guns and Roses cover of the song was a thousand times better, but that was one thing Glen and me always disagreed about. Of course I never thought about shooting him over this disagreement as I did about the terrible thing he said about Telecasters. I told Glen we would probably fit it in one of the prayer segments at the end of the show.

When she heard we were doing these songs, Anne didn't

complain about the planned costumes for "Hell is for Children," she just though it was a bad choice of songs and reflected badly on the family.   It was obvious that she was suspicious of "Carry On My Wayward Son" even without saying anything.   You could tell she thought it reflected something that should remain forever in the closet.

But she was furious at the choice of "Hymn 43."   I tried pointing out the singer keeps saying "Jesus save me" at least 5 times.   But on this point my words were wasted.   It was obvious that Anne believed more in the trappings of religion than to the spirit of any positive message a religion might have. In her opinion, the New Testament was mainly a condemnation against homosexuality and, most importantly, against Gay Marriage.   Of course, I've read the Bible from cover to cover and found very little against homosexuality, about the same amount as there is against eating pork or shellfish. Unfortunately, no one in the family read that much of the Bible, or if they did, was willing to argue with Anne about it. And since our projected audience had the same basic beliefs as Anne, it was probably for the best that any Biblical arguments be raised by Gene, who, in the end, would be discounted if only because he was black and a liberal.

If both Anne and Glen demanded that Billy not record *Hymn 43*, I would imagine that he would give in to them.   I told Billy that I'd write him a Christian Rock song, that he could take the credit for and say he wrote.   It would be something that would make them think again about *Hymn 43*.


Sinful Girl
by Billy Morgan

First Verse:
Oh why are you such a bad girl

So bad you just can't be saved
And why take so much pleasure
In being so eff-ing depraved.
I've guess you've always been a bad girl
Always been sinful through and through
You got a one way ticket to the bad place
And that's why I'm leaving you.

Chorus:
The Necrophiliac is kneeling
Oh! she's nodding to Death's Blade
She thought she had a free ride
But those plans have been misplayed
She almost wakes and wonders
Can this really be the end?
But goes on to the finale
As she greets her only friend.

Second Verse:
Oh you are such a sinful girl
Cause you're really bad in bed
And you're going to burn in hell girl
Cause you give lousy head.
Oh you are such a sinful girl
You never do anything right
When I asked you to lick the head
Why did you have to bite?

Chorus

Third Verse (Spoken)
Oh why were you such a bad girl?
You just could not be saved

You took way too much pleasure
And seemed to treasure being depraved.
Oh you were such a bad girl
You were sinful through and through
I really tried to save you but
But there was nothing I could do.

Chorus

Guitar Solo

Chorus

Billy wanted to change "bad in bed" to "wicked in bed" but without explaining why, I told him that would completely change the meaning of that part of the second verse. I did mention that, from a man's point of view, being wicked in bed was actually a positive trait. Of course, I wasn't sure if being bad in bed was actually sinful from a Christian point of view. . .

"You mean like your girlfriend Ms Laroux?" Billy asked.

"Maybe if she was fifty pounds lighter and—" I stopped myself from explaining the difference between domineering and playfully assertive. "And I wouldn't say she was my girlfriend. I know how you kids like to joke—"

"Yeah well she thinks she's your girlfriend," Billy said, now playing the puppet master, "and since she can pull the plug on the show at any time and have us thrown back in foster homes you better not disillusion her."

"Seriously, I think you're imagining things."

"Lindsey!" he called Lindsey over who had been doing something in the kitchen. "What's different about Ms Laroux since she's met uncle fatty?" [Uncle Fats shithead!]

"She wears makeup every time she comes around. And perfume. She dresses more nicely too. And she's nicer to mom and us.  She's even calling us by our right names."

"Are you sure she's not interested in Gene?" I asked.

They both laughed.

"She'd never fuck a nigger or a convict."

Then they school me about social distinctions, using the n-word three or four times as well as various references to white trash, class, and how Laroux perceived me as being both educated and of a higher class.  This Billy found funny.

"Mom may have told her that your college nick name was Colonel Carpet Muncher," Lindsey said, "but you can be damn sure she put more emphases on college than well, you know."

I didn't really know, but it seemed to explain why she came on so strong on our first two hookups.  And how different it was from the third time, when we made out for half a minute in the toilet before she blew me.  I didn't know which was the true Lucy, but she possibly wasn't a natural dominatrix or, if the kids are right about class distinctions, the sort of woman who goes around blowing men in toilets.  Now I, in some sense, felt really violated.  And it wasn't Lucy this time, it was Anne that I, no *we*, had to thank for it.

I decided to let Billy record "Hymn 43," but to not tell anyone about it.  That it was to be a surprise.  And I would go back to the original recording of the rap discussion and excerpt an image I was never going to use of Anne making a fist and insert it among all the bruising scenes in the "Hell is for Children" song, right before the line "they blacken your eye" and then flash to whoever wasn't singing that part showing them with a black eye.  Hell, I might even decide to change my mind about having Billy wear hot pants in the video, or maybe only in the part which shows him on crutches with bandages around one of his knees.  Hell, I'll even remove the teen prostitute aspect of it.  Just focus on physical child abuse.

I had, I believe, reached a catharsis in my thinking and I no longer needed to show Anne fighting with the kids.  I would show some of the more nasty shots I had of Anne and let the viewers make their own inferences.  But I wasn't thinking with my head, just following the dark recesses of my heart.

# Chapter 15 Domineering the Dominatrix or Cinni has a Clue

First things first, I would take Lucy out and apologize for the shabby way I treated her, taking her in the toilet and all that. Actually she followed me in there, even into the stall, initiating things, but that was beside the point. When I told her she shouldn't have had to just to get me to play on her [silly] song, she said she kind of enjoyed it. That it "reminded her of some of the crazy things she did in college."

"Like kissing your girlfriends for shots?" I asked.

"In college I went a little farther than that with a couple of the feminazis dykes. But not since my first year in college. And they were nowhere near as good as you."

"I guess a threesome in the future is out of the picture," I said, hopefully sounding like it was a joke.

"That would depend on who the guy is that you have in mind."

I wasn't sure if she was joking, though I laughed anyway and decided to change the subject hoping this didn't blow up in my face.

"Are you a big Rush Limbaugh fan?" I asked.

"Not really. That's one fat bastard that I really can't stand even when what he's saying is funny."

"Just wondering because you used his pet word for feminists."

"I only call feminist feminazis when they try to tell people *what to think,* or are just hypocrites, like those who will tolerate and even condone a lesbian for beating up her lover while condemning a man for doing the same thing. At least when the victim is a woman."

"I guess we're on the same page on some things."

I didn't care about any of this crap, but I knew how to play this game and could when it would benefit me.

I don't like talking that much about myself, but she asked

me if I ever had a homosexual experience, and I admitted, in strictest confidence, to the possibility that I might have been orally and/or anally raped by the I-10 Terminator.  I had been wearing some clothing when they found me, and the question had never been asked, not that I would have admitted to it then, even if I remembered it.  I never liked blackouts, but there are some things I would never want to remember, assuming any of it actually happened.  Five years later when the FBI questioned me, I was more willing to admit the possibility.  I added that just the fact that it might have happened and I didn't want it happening again, was one of the reasons I was able to quit drinking while I was still in my teens—thought it took me five more years to actually quit.

"I remembered some of Anne's sobriety papers were signed Fats B.  I had wondered if that was you?"

"A few times," I lied, knowing Glen had forged my name to her attendance sheet to prove she was going to meetings.  The fact that I hadn't been to a meeting in a year or two at the time didn't stop Glen.

"I usually never pay attention to who actually brings the sheet up to be signed.  I don't want to make them feel uncomfortable.  As long as they don't smell of alcohol or cause a disruption at the meeting."

"Is that where you met Glen, at an AA meeting?"

"Actually it was at an Online AA meeting where I was a host for a long time, starting on AOL.  We later moved to our own internet web site.  Someone we both knew talked us into moving down here and sharing a house to save on expenses.  She moved to New Zealand around a year afterwards.  I had some other friends down here who were also from New Jersey."

The evening ended, of should I say started, with me going over to her place for some old fashion relatively vanilla sex with just enough foreplay to keep things interesting.  I was willing to stay the night but she seemed concerned about what her neighbors would say about a strange car—a small pickup truck actually—in her driveway.  After doing her again, I went back to the asylum.

Only Cinni was up when I got back.  She was watching TV. Ordinarily, I don't watch much TV.  Before moving here, I didn't even have cable TV, just internet.

But since the movie Cinni was watching was *Tropic Thunder*, one of my favorite comedies, I sat down on the opposite side of the couch from Cinni, after making sure she was watching it and not going to start channel surfing.

She asked what I was up to, but I think she knew.

I told her that I took Miss Laroux out for dinner at Popeyes.

"And?"

And Cinni seemed really interested both in what happened with Laroux and in me.  Of course, she was probably just playing with me but I was past the age where playing with me was synonymous with playing with fire.  But that didn't mean that I didn't play too, though in my case I was playing along, rather than playing with.

She looked at her phone, not sure if she was checking for text or the time.

"Since you're not recording this," she asked, "would you mind if I took my Crazy Burger shirt off?"  And without waiting for a reply, she took off her uniform top exposing a nice yellow LSU sports bra.

"Glen buy you that?" I asked, reasonably sure that he didn't, being a big Texas A&M fan.

"I got them with my second or third Crazy Burger paycheck," she said.  Being as pretty as she was, she didn't have to contribute to the rent, electricity or utilities.  "Want to see the matching shorts?"  And again, without waiting for a response, she briefly stood up to let her pants slide to the floor showing what looked like yellow polyester shorts with the LSU logo. Not very tight or sexy but exposing a lot of thigh, which I nearly always find sexy. "Just remember it's OK to look, just don't touch," she added, smiling one of those smiles that seemed to say that touching might actually be a distinct possibility, though part of me knew it wasn't.

"You're certainly much better looking that Robert Downing Jr in black face."

"Huh?"

"You said it was OK to look so I'm looking and I am very much enjoying the view." It was still February, and even when it wasn't cold outside, most women still dress much more conservatively that they do in the late spring, summer, and early fall, when most women show a lot more skin.

"I mean," I added, "I'm not watching the TV even though it's one of my top 10 or 20 all time favorite comedies."

"Thanks, for watching. If mom wasn't going to be home soon I'd suggest that it'd be all right if you pulled your dick out and jerked off. I might even offer to give you a helping hand."

"As much as I'd enjoy a helping hand," I said, not having had sex in nearly half an hour, "I usually take a long time to finish with an old fashion. I'm much quicker when I'm getting blown."

"That's one thing I don't do. Period!"

I wasn't actually expecting her to give me a blow job, or even a hand job for that matter, but it sounded like she didn't even give her boyfriends blow jobs, which meant she was even more high maintenance than I thought she was.

"Not that you're my girlfriend or ever would be, I know you're way out of my league, but I don't think I ever went out with a girl for more than one or two dates without getting at least a partial blow job, even when they said they'd just give me a hand job."

"I'm just not any good at it. Which one is Robert Downing

Jr?"

Back to the movie. Back to reality too. I didn't know what kind of games Cinni was playing, but there was a part of me that was glad she changed the subject. I really wasn't sure of my relationship status with Lucy, but I was never comfortable being in relationships with more that one person at a time. I didn't mind the "cheating" part, but the keeping everything straight part was a major hassle that even data bases and spreadsheets couldn't handle.

Anne was pissed when she came home and saw Cinni in her underwear. And, of course, since Cinni was the one in her underwear, she was pissed at me.

"What the fuck you doing to Cinni?"

"We're watching a movie: *Tropic Thunder*; Ben Stiller, Robert Downy Jr., Jeff Black. Nothing more!"

"You got her half naked you pervert!"

"Mom, please!  You got to be crazy to think I'd have anything to do with Fats!"

"You have to be careful Cinni, he's a sick basturd.  If he'd fuck Laroux, he'd fuck anyone."

"Could you please leave Lucy out of this?"

"Lucy is it?  She wouldn't give you any so you try to seduce Cinni?"

"I just wanted to watch the movie!" I said.

"And you were going to put on porn afterwards?"

"Mother stop it!"  Cinni said loudly, "It was hot with the heat set so high so I took my uniform off. I'm wearing the same clothes that I'd wear outside if it was this hot outside. No one did anything wrong."

"Well no one better!" and she went to her room, but left her door open, perhaps so she could watch whatever it was she imagined we were doing.

There was another part of me that wanted to fuck Cinni now, not because she was attractive and had a killer body, but

because it would piss her mother off so much that she'd???
Shit, she might actually kill me!

"Let me talk to mom for a bit.   Explain that nothing
happened or was going to happen."

She went into her mom and Glen's bedroom and closed the
door.  I couldn't hear anything they said, and yes, there was a
part of me that wanted to listen, but after a few minutes Anne
started laughing hysterically.    Cinni came out shortly
afterwards, smiled, and said "everything's cool."

"What was so funny?"

"I told her about an April Fools prank I'm going to pull on
Billy.  And no, I'm not telling you.  You might tell him.  I
shouldn't have told her really, but I knew if she'd laugh then she
wasn't angry anymore."

I thought there was more to it than that, but being around
this lunatic asylum was enough to drive anyone a little
paranoid.  After the movie I took a shower to get what was left
of Lucy off me.  I usually wash my dick right after sex to avoid
disease, but I was fairly certain Lucy was clean in that sense,
or, at least, I hoped so.

After getting in bed I jerked off imagining myself with
Cinni on the couch with her LSU sports bra pulled up so I
could fondle and kiss her breast.  Then I fantasized about going
down on her, though for no where near as long as I had spent
earlier that evening going down on Lucy, then entering her and
fucking her brains out and having my third happy ending for
the night.  Now I just had to remember that it was Lucy I
fucked and Cinni I jerked off thinking about, but jerk off
memories were never as enduring as the real ones are.

I wasn't really sure if I liked Lucy, though she was a fun
fuck and I imagined we could find other things, even non-
sexual things, that we liked doing.  I doubt though, that I could
ever like Cinni.  She was close to a ten, almost certainly a nine.
But there never really seemed to be anyone home.    And

although Lucy might only be considered a five or six or maybe a seven if she lost around thirty pounds, there was definitely someone there—even if she was a liberal. I will say this much for Cinni, using only my imagination and, well, I guess, my hand, she seemed like a really good fuck.

In reality, I wasn't interested in Cinni. It was only the fact that she was near that made her desirable. Much worse was the knowledge that *Tropic Thunder* was ruined as a movie that I could watch over and over again. From now on, every time I watched it I'd think of Cinni, and, even worse, Anne nearly catching us. I have such a bad memory that I forget the jokes in a movie and can therefore laugh at them over and over again. My memory was good enough to remember that the movie was funny. But my memory wasn't bad enough to forget Anne and her toxic ravings.

# Chapter 16 Hell is for Ratings

We—Lindsey, Billy and me—secretly videoed 12 songs counting songs they covered separately. In addition to "Forgiven," "Hell is for Children," and "Hymn 43," they both did separate covers of "Satisfaction." We slightly reworded the third verse of Lindsey's version, so that she's trying to make some guy who says he'll do her when she's over her period. They did Smashing Pumkin's "Bullet with Butterfly Wings" alternating different parts of the verses and singing the "Rat in the Cage" chorus together. This was their best song, in some ways, I thought better than the original SP version, with their innocent sounding voices contrasting with the harsh angst and anger of the lyrics.

Lindsey did another Alanis Morrisette song, "You Learn," Soul Asylum's "Misery," and two by Nirvana: "All Apologies" and "Serve the Servants." Billy did Nirvana's "Man Who Sold the World." When I told him it was actually a cover of a David Bowie song, he YouTubed a bunch of Bowie's songs and said he wanted to do the version of "Putting Out Fire" with Stevie Ray Vaughn playing guitar, only with him playing lead guitar. I eventually overwrote the guitar parts, not really imitating or playing as well as SRV, but playing a million times better than Billy. Hopefully, Billy wouldn't realize the change. I'd have to work pretty hard to play as badly as Billy, who only new a hybrid variation of the first position of the Blue Scale, which he learned from Glen. I had told Billy several times, as I told Glen, that there was a second blue note on the third string, but the only flat fifth note that he used was the one on the fifth string.

Lindsey also did a grunge punk cover of Miley Cyrus' "Wrecking Ball" which was the only song they covered that wasn't originally released before they were born. She also considered doing Lady Gaga's "Poker Face," but I discouraged her saying it would be impossible to do a cover of it better than

Eric Cartman's cover of it from *South Park*, which she actually agreed with.  They both did covers of one of my songs called "Exit .38" which I thought of as a sentimentally sad song about friends who had committed suicide.  As much as I hate country, I actually once thought of releasing it as a country song. Fortunately Billy's version of the song worked out well as a ballad while Lindsey did it as an almost upbeat blues number with a fast tempo.  I tried to get them to do a cover similar to Izzy Dirtnap's version of "Paranoid," but neither was interested.   Lindsey wouldn't even consider covering Katy Perry's *I Kissed a Girl*, which I had previously pitched to Cinni and Brittney with the same results.  I tried to get them all to at least practice singing it, if only to create some magic between them and Anne.

I figured we had enough songs to release an extended single of Gospel songs, maybe even an EP and, if there was any demand, a CD, mainly of Rock songs.  And, more importantly, I was able to rewrite the Mardi Gras episode so that it appears that the last thing the kids, mainly Lindsey and Billy, wanted to do was see a "stupid parade" and at the end I added the video that I remade for the song "Hell if for Children."  I don't like to pat myself on my own back, but I thought this was brilliant and turned what was basically a boring show into possibly the best show of the season.  Admittedly, comparing child abuse with having to watch a parade might anger some victims of real abuse as well as Halestorm fans or the fans of Pat Bennitar (the Halestorm of the eighties with a higher vocal range).  I was banking on kids relating to it by identifying with having to do something they really didn't want to do but being "forced" to because their parents or teachers made them.  Hell, sometimes the agent of angst is just the person with the remote control, which is something even adults can relate to.

We just had to shoot a few more morning Serenity Prayer

scenes, which we may end up dropping, a few more dinner scenes, maybe a visit to Walmart or something like that for a little color. Have each of the kids followed by a cameraman, or camerawoman in the case of another of Cinni's friends who was willing to work for the minimum wage and wait to be paid until we were. The hook for the Walmart Episode was everyone got to pick their choice for supper one day a week, not going over twenty dollars. They all shopped individually and kept the change after checking out. As a result, some of them provided more for the family than others.

Reality:

Since Cinni always provided supper on Tuesdays, when Glen was usually asleep and Anne at work, she only had to feed 5 people including Granny. Nine times out of ten she would prepare store brand Pork and Beans ($1.50), Generic Hot Dogs ($3.00), Sauerkraut (.75) and either bread (0.88 cents) or Hot Dog Rolls ($3.75). After adding 7% sales tax, she usually pocketed around $13.50 when she bought bread, or $10.50 when she bought hot dog rolls. She usually bought bread.

Lindsey, who had Saturdays, had basically the same menu, but instead of getting Sauerkraut, she got Cheddar Cheese ($2.50). She prepared them differently, baking the hot dogs, which she split down the length of them around half an inch, on top of a baking dish filled with beans which she added a generous amount of brown sugar to, and when they were more of less done, she added cheese to all but two of the dogs because Granny was lactose intolerant, and baked them for another minute or two so the cheese would melt. Since she served them with rolls, she only took home about $8.50.

Billy, who had Mondays, always bought a really large frozen Lasagna, garlic bread and 3, 4, 5 or more bottles of Mountain Dew, depending on the price. He rarely had any paper money for change. He loved lasagna with garlic bread, and, he confided to me, he developed a taste for Mountain Dew when he found out none of his sisters nor his mother like it.

Among the children, Brittney, who had Sundays, was the only wild card, getting what she felt like at that time. Also, she always got desert, usually Ice Cream, Pie or Cake. And, quite often, the desert never made it to Sunday.

Anne, Glen, and sometimes Granny prepared supper on the other three days. Sometimes Glen would prepare breakfast, but usually the kids ate boxed cereal and on weekends made their own lunches with cold cuts or peanut butter and jelly or fluff.

Reality TV: Cinni got a Chuck Roast, with Potatoes, Carrots and Onions and a Pepperidge Farm cake for desert. Went over, no change.

Lindsey got a Packaged Cornbeef with Cabbage and Potatoes and cherry pie for desert. Went over, no change.

Billy, staying in character, got lasagna, garlic bread and Mountain Dew. Only a little change—no paper.

Brittney got Chocolate and Strawberry syrup and two and a half gallons of Ice Cream for what she liked to call Ice Cream Sundae Sunday. Went over, no change.

When they went over, they were supposed to pay out of their own allowance, but in this case I paid the difference with the understanding that the money would come out of what was not allocated from when we were finally paid. And with that, we got to record four meals being prepared for future episodes, and, of course, Cinni's was a complete disaster; she was able to destroy a pot roast while appearing very adorable.

Lindsey was smart enough to ask Glen to help her with the Crock pot Corn Beef and Potatoes adding the Cabbage during the last hour of cooking.

Billy didn't deviate from his usual, though when we recorded the family super he kept offering the girls Mountain Dew.

With Brittney everything went to hell. Her "dinner" was

held in the back yard.  Since she ate nearly half the ice cream before Sunday, I had to get more, and she also asked me to get bananas to make banana splits along with a couple cans of whipped cream and bottled cherries.  Not thinking, I got the kind of whipped cream that came with nitrous oxide.  I had, of course, heard of whippits, but I always thought it was an urban legend like getting high on coke and aspirin which I had actually tried and tried and tried, but after around 50 cokes and maybe a thousand aspirin, I gave up trying.  Since whipped cream was a lot more expensive, I never actually tried it figuring I'd be wasting my money.

Apparently Brittney and Lindsey, who were both at the same foster home picking up the same bad habits, knew differently.   And both apparently knew half a can wasn't enough to get them where they wanted to go and that the second can was worth fighting over.  Billy and Cinni broke it up and Cinni shook the can and then squirted out all the whipped cream into a few bowls while also releasing the remaining gas so that Brittney and Lindsey couldn't inhale it. This was all recorded but hopefully the viewers would think that they were fighting over whipped cream.  I'm sure though that some would probably know that the two kids were Nitrous Junkies or addicts or tweakers, or whatever the politically correct term or word was.  This was, for me anyway, the sad part of the day.  (I noted though that we might have to have a few rehab episodes in the future though not sure if rehab equaled ratings for our target audience but if not, maybe it would add a new ratings block of viewers.)   In retrospect, laughing gas probably was less damaging than huffing glue. Probably.

The fun part was when Granny slipped on a banana peel, falling fortunately on a shrub before rolling onto the ground and crying out that she broke her tits.  Instead of getting up, she offered to take her teeth out and give Billy the best blow job he ever had if he'd run to the store and get her a bottle of Night Train.   Billy who probably never had a blow job, but had probably been offered one by his great-grandmother on numerous occasions when she was too drunk to realize that he her nephew and was only thirteen, was smart enough to ask for the money first, at which point she offered to take her teeth out, etc., to Cinni and Gene, who was on the second camera.   They both asked for the money up front which pissed her off and she ended up crawling on her hands and knees to her trailer, rejecting all offers for help standing up.

The best part turned fun when Brittney started throwing scoops of Ice Cream at Lindsey, who picked it up and threw it back.  Pretty soon every one was involved in the food fight and they all lived happily ever after.

# Chapter 17 Night Train to Crazy Burger

We obtained permission to record an episode at the Crazy Burger where Cinni used to work. For that night, Cinni would return to work and all the kids would harass her and throw french fries at her, and each other. At a certain point, the manager would ask and then tell us leave. This was all scripted, of course.

Granny doesn't actually have a drivers license, but we pretended she did and that she drove Lindsey, Brittney and Billy to Crazy Burger. I made a deal with her that if she didn't drink before we drove her there, then I would give her a bottle of Night Train at the "restaurant" and two more after we finished recording and got her back to her trailer. I gave her the first bottle after she got out of the mini van I rented. I gave them each ten dollars to spend of burgers, fries, soft drinks, etc.

As expected, Granny got a large soda, went to the woman's bathroom, poured all, or most of the soda out, though keeping at least some ice, and filled the soda container with Night Train and then went to the booth the kids were at. When her number was called, Billy got her tray for her, which only had a large order of fries indicating she took home about six dollars in change. Everyone else made pigs of themselves taking home very little paper money.

Cinni's main task, tonight anyway, was cleaning up the tables after people left. As soon as she finished with a table, Brittney or Billy would make a little mess at the table, though not, of course, when Cinni was looking. The idea being not so much to make Cinni look incompetent, but just to give her a hard time and make her redo her work. And then Brittney "accidentally" dropped her soda and when Cinni was moping it up, Billy patted her on the back holding a stickum paper saying "D Student at Work!" which attached itself firmly to her back, as planned.

Granny lit a cigarette, ignoring the laws forbidding smoking

in restaurants.  (This wasn't scripted.)  Cinni came over and
said, trying to sound forcible:

"Put that cigarette out!  Now!"

"Well look who put on her big girl panties today!" Granny
said, sounding both offended and outraged.  "I got news for
you Miss Cinnamon March-April-May June Morgan hyphen
Carter.  I's a free country and we still have some rights."

"And if you don't put out that cigarette, you'll have the right
to a lawyer which you can't afford, the right to bail which you
also can't afford and a right to a phone call when they arrest
you."

"If she smokes can we?" a black woman at a nearby table
said.

"You go girl," Granny said.  "I marched with Marvin
Luther King to get you the right to vote and the right to smoke.
Now they want to take away our right to smoke and vote."  I
didn't think she was drunk enough, but then she started crying.

At this point the manager came over and asked them to
leave, saying that if we stayed, that he'd have to call the police.
We shut everything down and helped Granny out to the mini
van.  I went back in and apologized to the manager, who said it
was alright, that he actually wouldn't have called the police
until someone complained about the smoke, but didn't want to
be "filmed" saying that.  He added that someone lights up at
least once a week.

He then suggested that the kids could come back and we
could "film" them having a food fight which Cinni could break
up, though not before they threw their last fries at her.  This
was done, though it took a lot of work to edit it together with
the earlier scene.  The manager provided the fries though, so it
didn't cost us anything more.

I was thinking about recording Anne telling the kids to go
to Nawleans to watch the mardi gras parade and to have fun.  I

figured after around 25 or 30 attempts, she might look mad
enough so that she looked like an abusive mother which would
help round out the Mardi Gras episode.  Since Anne was far
from an abusive mother, in fact overly permissive on the verge
of spoiling her kids, I decided not to.  The only times she
seemed abusive were when she thought Billy might be, was, or
was becoming, gay.

I once jokingly asked her if I could take Billy to a sheep
farm so he could lose his cherry, but she replied that if I wasn't
so cheap, that I should take him to a cat house instead.  But she
didn't actually say no about the sheep. . .

As far as I could tell, we had the first season finished.  The
last four episodes would require more editing, but those we
could submit a week at a time, two weeks before they would be
shown.

One day while Anne was at work, I saw Brittney wearing a
black sweatshirt and black pants and decided to ask her if she'd
like to do a couple songs, if not for this season, then for next
season, or perhaps for the non-gospel CD, assuming we
released one.  She didn't particularly like the songs I choose,
but was willing to do them.  I had to change a few words of the
first verse, which she memorized and was listening through
headphones to the original recordings so she could sing in tune.

"Finished with *that moron* cause he could help *with my sick*
mind," Brittney sang.  The next line she replace "frowning"
with "*downing*," possibly not understanding the lyrics.  Other
than the mentioned changes in the first verse of "Paranoid,"
this cover was very similar to the Izzy Dirtnap version of Black
Sabbath's great song.  She also did the punk version of
"Communication Breakdown"" that I did with my early
nighties grunge/punk groups Blind Boner and Courtesy Flush,
She would have preferred doing the Zeppelin version, but did
mine instead, the main difference being that the lyrics in the
verses of my cover were completely inarticulate.  It wasn't any-

where near as good as my cover, but that was only because I was much better at being deliberately inarticulate than she was. Still, I'd give her an A for Effort.

Around this time, Glen told me he wanted to do a couple Kenny Roger's songs his father always used to listen to, "See the Condition my Condition Was In" and "Tell it all Brother." And he didn't want to make any changes to the songs using the same basic arrangements. The fact that his voice was not better than mine didn't seem to bother him. I didn't feel like learning the songs so we used karaoke version for the music for "Condition" but told him he'd have to play all the parts for the other song. As much as I hated country music, I could stomach Kenny Rogers, at least in small doses, but I didn't want to have anything to do with the recording process. I was extremely grateful though, that he didn't want to record "Coward of the County."

After listening to "Tell It All Brother" I relented and figured it could be interpreted as being close enough to gospel, that we could include it with our Gospel/Christian Rock EP. It was certainly better than any of the other gospel songs we did, not counting the not so Christian one I wrote for Billy, which probably wouldn't be included on the EP, though maybe on the Rock CD.

Just to be all inclusive, I wrote the following for granny which she seemed to like:

Every day
I kneel down and pray
That I get to ride the
Night Train home to Jesus.
Every night
I bathe in your sweet light
Knowing God is near
And that he loves us.

Chorus:
Before the world gets within
I spit out the seeds of sin
And even though I'm made of mud
We get the light God's love will bud
And with God's help we'll get above
We get the light, we get the love
And with God's help we'll rise above
We get the light, we get His love.

Every time
It feels like a crime
That some would ever miss the
Night Train home to Jesus.
Every one
Who wants to find the Son,
Can take Him in their heart
And know that He's with us.

There were a few inside jokes in the song, which she either ignored or didn't get.  I figured she was probably glad to be included in the Musical Morgan aspect of the show and, if we ever do make the EP, I wanted at least one songwriting credit on it, not that there was any real money in an EP or CD.  But, there might be some.

At this point, we were just waiting for the first episode to air.  March 19th seemed a long way away.

By the end of the first week in March, I had gone out with Lucy 4 or 5 times more times, out now being defined as going to one of our places, usually hers, for foreplay—cunnilingus—and sex—coitus—usually two or three times, ending, usually, without a lot of please-please-please begging on my part, with a blow job—fellatio.  Sometimes the blow job would come before the second and third screwing.  Sometimes not at all.

Otherwise, the rhythm was established though not without variation in sexual positions—missionary, cowgirl, reverse cowgirl, doggie style, kneeling and standing monkey style, and, one of my favorites, a variation of the Magic Bullet with her laying on a table or desk with her legs in the air.

As much as she loved receiving oral, I could never get her to sixty-nine with me, not after our first experience anyway, which was really just a 60 or a 9.   With actual sex, she preferred being on top, but didn't mind the missionary position, and loved the Magic Bullet once I talked her into doing it on her kitchen table.

And even though I think they are against the Law in Mississippi, she had an assortment of power tools.  Rather than supplementally using my fingers when going down on her, she asked me to insert her vibrator to the point she indicated—I imagine her G-spot—and then "go to work on" her clit, which I licked with the bottom of my tongue.

After climaxing, she told me to keep going, and she came two, three, four, five—I lost count after seventeen and we'd still be doing it if she had used Energizers batteries instead of Dollar Store ones in her plastic lover.  She told me she'd give me multiple blow jobs when it was "that time of her month," but when the time came, she just wanted to be alone.  Although I was looking forward to the blow jobs without begging, I solaced myself with the fact that I usually didn't have to beg, grovel or buy her things to get blown.  Usually I just had to go down on her and fuck her a couple times.  Sort of a win-win situation and, since I usually liked eating her pussy, I was able to throw in extra win.

I tried to get her to let me video her blowing me on my phone cam "just to have something to jerk off too," but she said that there was "enough porn on the web" to keep me entertained.  She managed not to state the obvious that she didn't want to join the legions of foolish ex-girlfriends, now amateur porn actresses.  She also mentioned the NSA, that they could access everything, including pictures and videos, on my phone and that she could lose her job and therefore be subject to blackmail if "those bastards had a video of me sucking a dick."  I wasn't 100% sure about the losing her job part, but I had no doubt about the abilities of the NSA and I no idea if the average NSA analyst had a high enough standard of morals to preclude blackmail.  Some people would do it just because others found it degrading.  In reality, it's probably a small percentage of men, and a much smaller percentage of women who would upload that garbage.  Of course, that wouldn't stop me from looking for amateur porn of Cinni or anyone of the thousand women I've met over the years—not that I've ever found any.  Or ever really expect to, just some similar to women I've known.

As the big night approached, someone realized that Morgan-Carter family would have to get a higher tier on their cable package and, of course, I was the only one with any money, so I had to pay for it.  Apparently someone had to flip a switch somewhere, but it was done in time so that the *Armed American Patriot Channel* was now available to us.

Since the channel changed its name, again, we decided to take a new Stock Photo of the family with most of the family holding a rifle or shotgun except Glen, who had an old Colt .45 automatic in his left hand, point up, in his right hand, cradled under his forearm, he held Dallas, his chihuahua.  Granny held what looked like a German potato masher grenade, which was, in fact, a potato masher.  Anne was wearing hand cuffs.  Gene, the only non-family regular on the show, was dressed like a security or prison guard and looking at Anne as if he was guarding a prisoner.

# Chapter 18 The Pilot Airs

On the night *The Morgan Family Rules!!!* debuted we invited both Lucy and Gene over, since Gene wasn't in that episode he came very reluctantly, mainly because he'd have to bring his own bottle since no one in the Morgan or Morgan-Carter family drank, nor would liquor be served. At least Anne wasn't supposed to as a condition of her parole, Glen didn't, and none of the kids had been caught drinking, though I wouldn't put it past them. Granny, aka Gram aka Gram Gram was a no show. She of course, drank, often to excess, but she wasn't allowed to drink in the house. We would have made an exception for her tonight, if we had thought of it. She was also a no show at supper, which wasn't unusual. I suspected that if no one saw her for a week or two then they might check her trailer to see if she was still alive. Then again, I wasn't sure if anyone really cared.

The show came on at 8:00pm Eastern Time—7:00pm our time. Everyone enjoyed the show!

The *Armed American Patriot Channel* ran a disclaimer before airing the show stating that the actions, opinions, values of the Morgan-Carter might not reflect those of everyone watching, especially those in Washington, and whether or not this channel supports their beliefs, we believe they have the right of free speech and that free speech is a right worth fighting for. It wouldn't be until the following morning before all hell broke loose.

They showed the half hour episode at 8pm, 9pm, 11pm and again at 4 am, all times in eastern time. At 7:15am Central time we were raided by an Army of Secret Service agents. Although many, well four or five anyway, were armed with M4's, Uzi's and MP5's, they weren't particularly aggressive. I sent a text to half a dozen people giving them the green light to call various news organizations including Fox News and all the major networks. That we were taken seriously by the Secret

Service was the best news I had since the program aired.

They questioned us all individually, often with two or three of their people present.  They seemed, of course, very interested in our intentions concerning the president.  I had told them all to say that the Obama targets at the shooting gallery was a publicity stunt to get liberals mad at us, though hopefully not so mad that they would boycott the show's sponsors.  Glen, Cinni and me, the only actual adults also stated that no one in their right mind would think that if we were serious, we would actually broadcast it.  Not if we were crazy enough to actually want to harm Obama.  And, of course, none of us would want to make a liberal martyr out of him.  Etc, etc, etc.

The Secret Service was still here when a few news vans actually showed up.  This was like waking up thinking you were having a wet dream only to realize that your girlfriend, wife, partner, whatever was waking you up with a blow job.

The only one of us who actually seemed dangerous was Brittney, who  kept affirming that Obama was the Antichrist and is in the process of destroying America.  I was sure she knew better, at least I hoped she did.  But she kept at it, playing potential assassin.

"Just look at the evil Obama-care has caused," said Brittney, who along with Granny were the only members of the family collecting medicaid.  I didn't think the Secret Service would arrest Brittney, but it would have been nice publicity if they took her somewhere wearing handcuffs, for further questioning and she was shown in cuffs being taken away on the news.

When they questioned me, I offered to sign an oath stating the target range scene was just a publicity stunt.  That I didn't believe most of the right wing "propaganda" about Obama.  I even added that I thought he had good taste in women, or possibly transvestites or transsexuals and that, if I was still drinking, I would probably let Michelle blow me even if she was a trannie. "Not that I ordinarily have sex with transvestites or transsexuals," I added. "Hell, I'll even reciprocate if she has a real pussy down there." I was trying to make them believe that I was stupid enough to think that I thought the First Lady would want to have a shag session with a fat slob like me.

Fortunately they didn't shoot anyone or arrest me when they left. Unfortunately they left without arresting anyone.

But we made a big splash and would have several hundred times as many viewers for out next episode. I was counting on a visit by the Secret Service but didn't think it would be so quick and probably only by one to two agents. After they left, we tried to get a press conference going, but the only member of the press who was still present owned a local free paper called the Hancock County Swapper—or maybe Swamper—which consisted mainly of want ads of items people wanted to sell. There were actually between 8 and 10 or so neighbors, all black, standing around watching the show.

The Hancock County Swapper reporter asked: "Do you really want to shoot Obama?"

"Of course no—" I started saying but was interrupted by one of my neighbors shouting:

"Baba Booey, Baba Booey!"

Even though there were no TV cameras or even radio reporters there. The Hancock County Swapper reporter did have what seemed to be a digital recorder though.

"Of course no—" I tried again, this time interrupted with:

"Rara Retard, Rara Retard!"

"NOT!" I shouted.

"No need to shout. Everyone can hear you.

"Mama Monkey!"

These interruptions got some laughs from those gathered around, even though I doubted they understood the Howard Stern show references. I doubted even the most hard core Stern fans still shouted out "Baba Booey" anymore, even when there was a suitable news conferences. But I recognized the long arm of Karma rebounding on me by remembering doing the same thing to Gary Dell'Abate, the real Baba Booey, as he tried to interview someone waiting in line at one of Howard Stern's book signings in Manhattan. The only difference being I was trying to make background noise, while not drowning them out. It took the last comment about not needing to shout, followed by 'Mama Monkey' to get me to start laughing too. . .

That afternoon I called the Armed American Patriot Channel to see if there were any negative ramifications and the person I talked to, the executive vice president of communications or something like that said everything was good and that they would send us a check for the first show directly. He said it would be larger than expected because of all the times they re-ran the episode. He said that they were getting a lot of complaints, but that they were good complaints, without actually explaining what good complaints were. He added the rap episode was bound to cause a lot more controversy and that the network would use the race card to "defend Billy against a bunch of liberal racists." He added that they had decided to keep running the pilot throughout the week until they ran the next episode.

I checked Facebook later and found that although a few conservatives loved the show, Liberals were just starting to get angry about the target range scenes, but I found links to that scene all over YouTube. I kept the two black off duty Police women in it, even though they didn't sign releases. I managed to edit it so that when they were swearing at me, it looked like they were harassing Brittney—not that she didn't aggravate them by calling Obama the Antichrist—and it got to the point where Brittney seemed the victim.

It couldn't have played out better. I just hoped that we wouldn't alienate any of our viewers with the following week's Rap episode.

The kids missed half a day school that Friday, but went late anyway. I told them to say that they were late because the Secret Service was too stupid to recognize an obvious publicity stunt—another example of how our government wastes our tax dollars. Lindsey and Billy said they would even lie—at least I think they were lying—by saying they actually liked—and Billy added respected—Obama. Of course, they were at that age when they might have said they liked him just to challenge their mother's political values. And maybe they really liked him.

Cinni showed up at work just to check the "buzz" as she called it. Since she wore her Crazy Burger uniform on the episode, she was now drawing full pay even though she was on, what she called personal leave. None of the workers there or the customers mentioned anything, but the manager was proud of her and changed her job description from server-custodial maintenance to Assistant Manager-server-custodial maintenance. Unlike some other fast food places, Assistant Managers there were actually in charge when the actual manager who, in this case, was the franchise owner, wasn't there.

Cinni was the only one who had a positive experience as a result of the show that day. Even though the kids all had signed excuses by their mother, they nearly all drew attention for being late. Much worse, none of the other kids in school recognized their new found fame, which negated it in all but their own minds. When they got home they were all pissed, and I was the target of their piss streams.

"Give it time," I said. "Wait until the season is over and goes into repeats. They've changed their scheduling so that they are going to show the pilot at least twice a day for the next week and then once a day for the following week while they rerun Billy's rap episode."

"I could almost feel it," Lindsey said.

"Me too," Billy said. "I want it now."

"The channel is very happy with the show. They may even decide to keep it at eight o'clock. I admit I was hoping the Secret Service raid would have drawn more publicity. But we can't have everything. Do you have any idea how lucky you are to even have a reality show?"

None of them replied to this, though Billy seemed to ponder several wisecracks.

"Most shows take years to develop, but this show was only conceived around 7 or 8 months ago and we're already on cable." Actually, I had first thought of this show when Glen first mentioned that the kids were worse, or more white trash, than the "Honey Boo Boo" family, but they didn't need to know that. And it was only a passing thought.

"Maybe I shouldn't tell you this, and please don't tell Anne, Glen or Cinni," I went on, "but right after the rap episode airs, we're going to upload an uncensored, low audio quality copy of Billy doing "My Wiggaz" to YouTube. Were also going to include links so people could purchase the high quality downloads of 'My Wiggaz.' Don't get me wrong, there's no real money in downloaded music, but it's another way of publicizing the show. I'm not saying it's going to, but there is a possibility of it going viral." This was a complete uncensored version with Cinni pretending to play the keyboards and Liz at her two piece drum kit wearing the red wig, the heart shaped sun glasses, the crop top faded denim jacket with a three inch diameter "I ♥ white trash" button over her left breast and, written on her fat belly in firetruck red lipstick "Love Child" while wearing matching, hi top faded denim shorts and looking a lot fatter than she actually was. While Billy rapped, Lindsey and Brittney stood on either side of him trying to look tough, like part of his posse or crew.

I didn't tell them that I was also considering uploading the family argument they had while making the episode. Glen's comment about Billy not knowing what a blow job was even with a dick in his mouth and granny telling him to spit would definitely go viral. But since they were trying to pretend to be a Christian family, I thought it might have a negative effect that could not be turned into a positive.

Anne had to work from 3pm to 11pm that Friday. I decided to stay up until she got home to see if she had heard anything at the Walmart where she worked at. As it turned out, several people did recognize her from the show. One older man, complaining about loosing his food stamps, even offered to drive her and the kids to Washington for some "Target Practice." If she could chip in on the gas, he added.

For once, she actually seemed happy. It almost felt weird not having her in some way angry at me, which she seemed to be since I first pitched this project—this show. That doesn't mean she didn't still regret renting me the room at their place. And probably a part of her regretted the situation their family was in which forced them to rent the room so that they wouldn't lose the house. I never questioned if the idea of asking Cinni to contribute to the household expenses ever occurred to her. Glen was probably too pussy whipped to bring it up. The one thing I remember him telling me about Cinni when they first met was that she loved spending money.

As long as she was happy, that was the main thing. She wouldn't be happy when she saw the Mardi Gras episode in two weeks. At least I think she would be mad. I was pretty sure I wouldn't be able to sell her the idea that she was acting in the "Hell is for Children" video segment. The important thing was that we could sell others outside the family that, of course she was acting, and damn good too, even if it is an unscripted reality show.

It was really just a music video segment rounding out an otherwise boring episode. No need to make more out of it. I was sure Anne was going to go ballistic and I was already rehearsing replies.  Could I still change it?  Probably.  Was I going to change it?  Probably not.  Sometimes art was more important than argument, I philosophized, not actually believing the crap I was rationalizing, but using it to justify an action that I believed was indefensible.  After this mental masturbation session, I finally ejaculated the following premise that maybe this was my way of bringing a little "real world" reality into a not very realistic program.  *Yeah, that's the ticket*, as Jon Lovitz would say.

Of course, my concerns weren't Anne's feelings, or the feelings of anyone else.  I just didn't want anyone important to the show to quit.  This was my way out from being a fourth rate literary hack.  My best selling book, *Polish Joke*, was both literally and figuratively a joke and even I knew it was derivative of the Elaine Evonavich's 'Stephanie Plum' books, even if I would never admit it.  My musical aspirations were even more dismal especially considering I haven't been able to sing sustained notes since I quit smoking in 1998.  This was my way out and I was committed.

# Chapter 19 Lindsey's Dark Secret

A little more hell broke loose after the second show. Billy came home from school with a big smile, a black eye and three hickeys on his neck. Cinni asked:

"Did your boyfriend give you those hickeys?"

"I got into a make out session with three different girls in the cafeteria at lunch. I got two of them at the same time. The ex-boyfriend of one of the girls hit me, but before I could hit him back, the girl jumped him and beat the crap out of him. All three girls said they would invite me to the next Sadie Hawkins dance."

"Fatty Frankenstein," Cinni said to me, "you've created a monster!"

"I'm happy for you Billy," I said, winking at him. "The last time I had three girlfriends—hell, I never had three at the same time!" I shook my head. "Damn!" I started laughing, actually happy for the kid even hoping he might have a foursome in his near future, though not sure he could handle three at the same time. For that matter, I didn't even know if he could handle one of them or was even old enough to come. . .

If Cinni wasn't there I would have told him to use protection. Knowing the families right wing attitude against birth control, I wasn't about to get them, mainly Anne of course, pissed off because I was concerned about Billy catching anything. At least not if we couldn't make an episode about it. I was actually concerned about his health and didn't want him to get VD and made a mental note to tell Billy sometime in the future to use a condom when messing with any girls who seemed to know what they were doing, at least for vaginal or anal sex. . . Actually, I think I forgot to tell him.

No one in the Morgan family probably cared if he got a girl or even all three girls pregnant. Mississippi led the country in teen pregnancies and it wasn't unheard of for a kid his age to knock up three girls. Even worse, it wasn't even controversial, at least as long as the male was in the same age range.

More importantly it would prove to his mother that he wasn't gay. Of course, what was good for the Morgan family wasn't necessarily good for the *Morgan Family Rules* and the dynamic between homophobic Anne and sexually confused Billy was good for the show, even if he wasn't all that confused.

Earlier in the day, using the somewhat silly YouTube handle MorganFamilyDude, I uploaded a video we made of "My Wiggaz" along with a link to download much higher sound quality mp3 version of the song. The YouTube version left out the verse about Uncle Fats being a great guy, which was only kept in the original because I wasn't a good enough video editor to delete it without messing it up and I hadn't yet entirely decided on not being an onscreen character. In this version, the first five verses are repeated and the second time the sixth verse is rapped, I changed it to:

My younger sista she has big tits   (My Wiggaz)
My older sista she got nice tits (My Wiggaz)
My twin sista she got no tits (My Wiggaz)
Big tits (My Wiggaz)
Nice tits (My Wiggaz)
No tits (My Wiggaz)
No tits (My Wiggaz)

(and starts to fade with the following repeated three and a half times)

Big tits (My Wiggaz)
Nice tits (My Wiggaz)
No tits (My Wiggaz)
No tits (My Wiggaz)


In this version Brittney and Lindsey added their voices to the "My Wiggaz" parts in the loop. Lindsey was really pissed at the rewording of the last verse that concerned her breast size. In this case, I took full responsibility for it, even lying and saying Billy was against it too—he wasn't against it and laughed for nearly a minute, when he first saw the rewritten verse. But just as I wanted tension between Anne and Billy, I wanted to keep the twin bond close between Lindsey and Billy, eventually, perhaps even appearing incestuous though only to the point where people might believe that they would have threesomes with bi-sexual of both sexes. Not that they would ever be that close. Only that they appeared to be that close for the pervs in our projected audience who like that kind of crap.

After the first episode, liberals would be watching the show. Billy struggling with homophobic Anne was one of the hooks we could use to actually make the program seem relevant. And incestuous twins? This was every liberals wet dream. And you could be damn sure those liberals who were fixated on "no tits," were also looking at Lindsey's points under the t-shirt she wore in the video, the pervs.

To console Lindsey, I showed her some old music videos of Brittney Spears which could best be described as before (the surgical enhancement) videos. Even before, Brittney Spears' breasts were bigger than Lindsey's, but it was obvious that there was also an after—implants. And that was always an option, I explained, assuming her breasts didn't grow larger as they almost certainly would. I added that:

"There were a lot of liberals out there who liked small breasted women."

"Really?" sounding not very convinced.

"They like small breasts and thin women."

I doubted there was any truth in this—the small breast part, anyway. On the other hand, liberals, conservatives and moderates—if they still exist—all preferred thin women. If liberals were, on average, thinner than conservatives, it was probably because they were more likely to be vegetarians or vegans and took in fewer calories because the food they ate was inedible. Maybe in a second season episode Lindsay could become a vegetarian, or a vegan. Then, maybe along with Billy, Lindsey could become Anne's second worse nightmare, a liberal! Assuming there was going to be a second season. I wasn't even 100% sure that all six of the remaining episodes we made were going to be broadcasts.

"Maybe next season I can come out of the closet, so to say," Lindsey said, breaking my train of thought. "That would really get mom pissed!"

"It certainly would, no where near as pissed as if Billy was gay, but she'd be mad as hell." One of Anne's best friends was a lesbian and they may even have had something going on sexually when they were in prison together, according to something Glen told me shortly after he started dating Anne.

"I'm not a lizbian fool! I'm a liberal, not that mom needs to know. [Deja vu again!] Have been since I was in the foster home and started watching Rachel Maddow on MSNBC."

"Actually, Rachel Maddow is a lesbian. She's been out of-"

"I don't care about that shit. Calling her a lizbian, whether she is one or not, is just a way you conservatives try to discredit her. That crap doesn't work with me." She went on for 4 or 5 minutes talking about how great Rachel Maddow was, yada-yada-yada. She even seemed interested in crazy liberal issues like human rights, women's rights, even civil rights. If she had mentioned animal rights I would have pitched the idea about her becoming a vegetarian. I could now understand why she refused to postulate that Obama was behind 911—"perhaps even flying one of the planes"—during one of the family's dinnertime discussions.

As far as the great Rachel Maddow was concerned, I wanted to tell Lindsey that Maddow was just another tool of the corporations that own the media. There was only one source of real information and that was on the internet. If she wanted the truth, she should watch Alex Jones who was exponentially more honest than even Fox News. Or, if she wanted real left wing propaganda, she should watch or listen to *Democracy Now*, Thom Hartmann, or Bill Press or a few other left wing tools that I suggested Gene follow to get some good talking points that we could deride on the show.

I could also have confided in here that I was pro-choice—just don't tell Anne!  But I usually only talked about being pro-choice with women who were similarly inclined and who I wanted to be intimate with and, in Mississippi anyway, it would still be 2 years and 17 days before I could be legally intimate with Lindsey.  Of course, no amount of figuring could suggest any kind of possibility where she'd want to have any kind of sexual relations me.   That's not to say that I was actually interested in her.  I wasn't.  Her legs were too thin!  The only one in that family that I was interested in was Cinni who was a lot prettier and had really nice tits, but I projected my chances with her as being zero to the power of infinity.  In other words, impossible.   On the other hand, I was always horny and, therefore, always looking, if not actually hunting.

I asked her to please try to keep her liberal political beliefs secret until we were ready to record it.   That it would make some great episodes.  We also wanted to catch her mother unprepared, that Anne's firework displays equaled ratings.  I even complimented her on her intelligence citing (liberal biased, I'm sure) statistics that liberals were, on average, smarter than conservatives.

# Chapter 20 Pay Day

The following Monday, March 30th, I received by registered mail a check for $100,000 for the first two episodes. I deposited it at the bank where I had set up our corporate account, but I was told I would have to wait until it cleared, probably by noon the next day, before the bank would produce checks for the amounts I wanted to write. The next day I had $10,000 checks produced for Arthur, our executive producer, Glen, Anne, Cinni, Lindsey, Brittney, Billy and me; $4,000 checks were made for Lucy Laroux, Beatrice Williams Graham (aka Granny, Gram and Gram Gram) and Gene O'Hara. I also withdrew $1200 in cash to split mainly between Buddy and Chris with a few hundred going to a couple of Cinni's friends who helped with video recording on several occasions. Around $5000 went to creditors leaving the corporation with a little more that $900, most of which would probably be used for taxes. The checks for Lindsey, Brittney and Billy were also made out for Anne Morgan Carter and had to be co-signed by her.

I didn't tell anyone, but I had been starting to get worried because it seemed to be taking so long for the check to arrive. Even after I got the check, I still thought I might bounce. Might, not would. . . Unknown to anyone in the Morgan-Carter family, I had a deal with Arthur so that I could buy him out if I gave him my five share dividends of the first episode. He was worried that something might go wrong and didn't want to be accountable in any way, thinking more along the lines of being associated with the *criminal activities of some of the cast* which wouldn't be covered by any limited corporate liability laws. He had his own business to run and didn't really think the show would last. Corporately speaking, I mainly wanted his shares as leverage when voting. He could have also been thinking that Anne, the Vice President of Morgan Family Rules, Inc., might get busted dealing or making meth, and even if the corporation was dissolved leaving him liable only to the amount he had invested, he might be accused of being a conspirator of her criminal activities—not that she was involved in any—though it is possible that I put some of these thoughts in his head while venting that I was nervous about how things might turn out. In any case, he got back more than twice what he put into it. He was now only a figurehead—an Executive Producer, in name only.

I got back to the zoo before Anne left for work and gave her her check and, since she asked for the other checks, I gave the three younger kids checks to her, even Glen's. All but Cinni's and granny's checks. I knew Cinni would just waste the money and Granny would drink her's up, but they were both adults.

She wanted both Cinni's and Granny's checks too. But when I asked why, she didn't answer. I could understand her not trusting me and I couldn't blame her for that. She told me she was going to leave early for work so she could deposit the checks and she seemed really flustered when I told her the kids would have to endorse them too before they could be deposited and that it wouldn't be a good idea for her to take them to work since there would be a 45 day wait if they were lost before they could be reissued. I wasn't sure if this was true, but I didn't want her going around Walmart showing everyone the checks in case they were stolen and cashed before a stop payment could be issued. Admittedly, I didn't trust Anne anymore than she trusted me. I asked her if she wanted to call Cinni and let her know "we" had her check, and when Cinni got home around 10 minutes later I let her hand her the check which she quickly went out and cashed.

I asked her if she wanted to come with me to Granny's trailer and hand her the check too, and she did. Anne knocked on Granny's trailer door, and when she didn't answer, she opened it and walked in. Granny was on the left side of the trailer sitting in front TV—she had a coaxial cable coming from the cable splitter inside the house.  She could have been sleeping, if she wasn't dead drunk or just dead.  Anne cleared her throat three times, each time a little louder, before Granny heard her.

"Here," Anne said, "we got something for you.  It's nearly four times what Social Security gives you every month."

"What?"

"We got your check for the first two episodes of the show.  Four thousand dollars."

That seemed to wake her up.

"Please," I implored, "don't spend it all on Night Train Express!"

"Don't worry sunshine.  I've given Night Train up for lent.  The only thing I drink now is tea and Kool Aid."

On the right side—front end—of the trailer as a kitchen dining area and on the table were about 20 or 30 Night Train bottles.  She saw me looking at them and said:

"Those have tea and Kool Aid in them.  I believe in recyling."

When we were walking back to the house, I said to Anne: "I'm glad she's drinking tea and Kool Aid instead of wine."

Anne laughed derisively and replied: "You really are a moron, you fuckin' idiot.  She may have given up blowin' ninety year old blind niggers for lent, but she still drinks as much as she ever did.  For as long as I can remember she's made wine out of tea mixed with sugar, yeast, fruit juice, lemonade and once it's fermented, she flavors it with Kool Aid.  She only drinks store bought wine to get the taste of cum out of her mouth."

The God fearing Morgan-Carter Family. . . I love this crazy family almost as much as I love paying taxes!

That night I brought Lucy her check.  I was hoping we could celebrate finally getting paid by having a heavy duty sexual marathon, but she begged off, saying she wasn't really in the mood.  Knowing how to get me off quickly, she did give me a rather vanilla blow job.  But I could tell it was only to thank me for delivering her cut.  She did tell me that she'd probably see me tomorrow and maybe we could celebrate then.  Before I left she asked me:

"Are we a couple?"

"I think so.  I mean I hope so."  I was a little confused.  "You mean exclusive right?  Like what they call 'going steady' in old 50's, 60's and maybe even 70's TV shows?"  I didn't want to use the word *serious*.

"Yes."

"I haven't asked you to get in a threesome have I?" I said, adding: "I admit I thought about it when I thought you were bi, maybe even fantasized about it.  But I never really seriously considered it."

"That's not what I'm talking about.  Are you having sex, any kind including oral and anal with any other women?"

"No," I said, though I tried not to answer too quickly.  Though I didn't want to appear to be thinking about it either.  "And I'm not fucking any men, or boys either, though Anne probably thinks I'm messing with her son."

"Anne's an idiot.  I just want to know if we're a couple."

I assured her we were—not that I was ready to commit to marriage at this point.  Given more time, who knows. . . (Actually, I never had sex with anyone more than 3 or 4 times where the idea of marriage still seemed practical.  Though there was no need to tell her that, especially considering I wasn't even sure I liked her.)

That seemed to ease her mind, not that I even try to pretend to understand women.  I tried to cop a feel of her breasts as we kissed goodnight, but she clutched my forearm, shook her head and said: "Tomorrow."

When I got back to the Morgan Maniac Preserve, Anne was in a good mood and invited me to celebrate with them tomorrow morning.   After picking Glen up from work, they would take the family out for a celebratory breakfast.   And not at Mickey D's either, they were sparing no expense and were going to the International House Of Pancakes in Gulfport. Apparently this was a big deal for them.   Even better than breakfast at Denny's.   I thanked her but said I'd probably sleep late.

# Chapter 21 April's Fool

I was awoken the next morning at around a quarter to seven with Anne shouting at everyone to "Hurry the fuck up," and that she ". . .had to pick up Glen at work" and to someone: "But you have to go, this is our big day sweetheart" and "Well Billy needs to take a shower, one of you girls can wait until we get back" and "No school today. We have to go to the bank and open accounts for you to start your college funds." This went on for around 10 minutes, then I heard the front door close, the car start, and drive away. It wasn't until they drove away that I realized that I might be able to get some good "footage" from their celebration. But it was too late now. Besides, an occasion at McDonald's would be much more realistic of the seedy white trash atmosphere I wanted to perpetuate for the Morgans.

At this point, I heard someone moving around in the house, though not making much noise. I doubted it was a burglar. Probably Granny or the "sweetheart" who apparently didn't want to go to IHOP. I grabbed my pistol-grip short barrel Mossburg, and went out to investigate, wearing only my boxer shorts, a t-shirt and flipflops. Cinni, wearing her LSU shorts and sports bra, was making coffee. She turned and saw me holding the shotgun aimed upward at around a 45 degree angle and said:

"It's alright if you want to shoot me. Life has no meaning anyway. Just be quick about it." Then, changing the subject, she asked: "Want me to make you some coffee?"

"Sure," I said, nodding. I then added, looking at the shotgun: "Let me put this away. If I let you talk me into killing you, it won't be here. And certainly not with a shotgun."

I went back to my room, stowed the shotgun behind the headboard of my bed, and put on a pair of bluejeans. It would be almost impossible to go back to sleep after the adrenal rush I got from the possibility that I might be facing a burglar—even though I didn't think there was one.  I grabbed a coffee mug which I use daily and haven't washed since I got it in 2011, and went back to the kitchen.

Seeing I was wearing jeans, Cinni said: "You didn't have to change.  Mom won't be back for at least three hours unless they change their mind and go to the IHOP in Slidell, which is probably closer, but it's still thirty or forty minutes away."

"Why didn't you go?" I asked, not really caring, though hoping I sounded concerned.

"I would have started binge eating like Brittney does and like her, I'd stop caring about my looks and start putting on massive layers of fat, no offense Fats.  Maybe I'd even start drinking like Grammy or doing drugs like mom used to."

"Food would probably do less damage, in the short term anyway," I said.  "I don't know that much about addiction, other than alcoholism, but meth and crack are, at least I've heard, very hard to kick—especially meth.  I strongly suggest not doing drugs harder than Marijuana.  And if you're going to drink, try to drink in moderation—not that I ever did.  Not after the age of eleven anyway."

"I hadn't thought about marijuana.  But won't that make me eat more?"

"Yeah, but when you're high you won't care.  But people do get addicted to marijuana too.  If I was a pretty girl like you, and please don't tell your mother I said this—and, I'm not trying to hit on you or anything like that—but if I was a pretty girl like you, and I had to get addicted to something, I'd become a sex addict."

"I could do the bunny sex stuff your Ann Lip always does, and just get done all over the place like her using 20 or 30 sexual positions.  But when some cute guy goes down and me and then asked me to do them with my mouth, I have a problem," she said.  "My boyfriends all break up with me and my last boyfriend actually told me he was breaking up with me because I was orally retarded and gave really bad blow jobs."

"You mean like your teeth were causing problems?"

"When I asked what I was doing wrong, he said everything. But he did keep telling me to watch my teeth."

"Did they have really large penises?   I mean girth not length?   So that they couldn't fit in your mouth without scraping either the upper or lower teeth or both?"   I couldn't believe I was having this conversation. I've had some bad blow jobs in my life, and at least two oral virgins who had no idea what to do but I never spent much time talking about it. Certainly not with a woman I was attracted to. That she was inversely attracted to me—completely disgusted, most likely— was, of course, obviously apparent to me.

"No.   I think most of my boyfriends were average.   Five, six, seven inches. . ."   She then went on for a few minutes describing more about her various boyfriend's cocks than I would ever want to hear.   The only guy she thought who ever finished in her orally apparently had a ten or eleven incher and, forcibly deep throated her, finishing in her throat.   She said it hurt worse than anal sex used to and after that one experience, she avoided him like the plague, and only dated him four or five more times.

Up until this point, I had nearly four and a half inches of a raging hard on.   Upon hearing this, my cock turtle-shelled and all interest in sex dissipated.   Before that I could almost taste her pussy and on the right side of my brain I visualized fucking her while she laid on the kitchen table with her legs at a ninety-five degree angle and her ankles resting on my shoulders.   But this fantasy faded fast while my conscience and concern took over my thinking apparatus.

I suggested maybe becoming a sex addict wasn't such a good idea; adding that before the first date, or hooking up, or hanging out or whatever she did with her future boyfriends, that she could tell the guys that she didn't perform oral sex.   If she wasn't so religious, I said, she could lie and tell guys her gag reflex caused you to vomit when more than the head was in your mouth and that you found the taste of semen disgusting.

"Wouldn't they know I was lying after I licked up their cum after giving them a hand job?"

Dishonesty wasn't going to work here.

"Maybe," I suggested, "You could go New York, or maybe much closer, in New Orleans, and find someone who has blow job classes." This is something I heard about from someone who liked the series *Sex in the City*. I also saw what looked like a blow job class conducted by an obvious homosexual in some silly comedy movie—not that it had anything to do with the movie.

At this point I had a brain storm while simultaneously a light seemed to appear in her eye and she said:

"Could you teach me?"

"Teach you what?" I asked, preoccupied with my own thoughts.

"How to suck di—, how to do fellatio? Slowly explain what I'm doing wrong and how to correct it."

This is not the sort of thing I even fantasized about, at least not with pretty women like Cinni. Even though I would already have had my dick out if she had asked me this before telling me about being deep throated the way she was, I found it hard generating interest. Somehow the focus had changed from extremely sexy and pretty to very young and vulnerable.

"To teach you I'd have to let you practice on me, and I know you don't want to suck my dick," I lectured.

"I do," she said, though I was pretty sure she was lying. "I really do."

"You may want to learn how to do something, but I'm not the one to teach you." Actually, if I wasn't sure she'd eventually regret it, or that her mother might find out about it and kill me, I'd let her practice on me forty or fifty times until she was a certified blow job queen.  But I was predominately thinking about the show.  Even when we weren't currently recording, I was always thinking of the show.

"Please, just for a few minutes?"

"You may think you want to, but you'll end up regretting it."

I thought about asking her to take off her sports and letting me see her nipples.  I might have changed my mind if they were hard.  Before I could say it, she said, rather loudly:

"It didn't work.  You can come out!"

At this point, Glen and Anne's bedroom door opened and Anne, Glen, Billy, Lindsey, Brittney, and even Gene came out into the family room and approached the Kitchen.

"What didn't work?" I asked, though I had a few guesses, they wouldn't have been as bad as what Cinni planned.  Definitely not what Anne added to it.

Around ten seconds after Gene came out of Glen and Anne's bedroom, one final person came out.

"I'm sorry," Lucy said and she approached me.  "I told Anne it was a stupid, immoral prank.  And I would have revoked her parole if Cinni had succeeded in getting you to whip your dick out or take your clothes off and allowed Lindsey and Brittney to see it."  *And I would never have anything to do with you ever again if you had,* she didn't have to add.  Lucy hugged me, kissed me a few times, though not on the mouth and then whispered: "I am sorry.  Really sorry."  She whispered more, but I couldn't hear over:

"She wasn't really going to blow you," Billy added.  "And she was lying when she said she was bad at it.  Buddy and Chris both said she gave really good blow jobs.  Buddy said she could suck—"

"Enough Billy!" Anne yell, sounding extremely angry.  "You shouldn't never disrespect your sister that way!"

"Well if I had known it was going to happen I'd be the one

saying April Fools because I would have told him everything and then the joke would be on you.

"Now can we go to Ihop?" He asked, adding: "Or was Ihop an April Fools joke too?"

"Can you take them honey dew?" Glen said. "I have to get some sleep before work tonight."

"Gene, Lucy, Fats you want to go to Ihop with us?" Anne asked, as if nothing had happened. "It's on me." She added, smiling.

I wanted nothing more to do with the Morgan family that day and Lucy felt the same way. Gene took Anne up on her offer and they all rode in Gene's new (used) mini van which he was able to put a down payment on using part of the $4000 that he got yesterday. Apparently he cashed the check with the Used Car dealer, getting around $2200 back in cash.

"Glen," I said after Gene drove away, "your family might not be as bad as 'Honey Boo Boo's,' but they are certainly weirder."

"I wanted to put a stop to it, but then Anne would have withheld sex from me for a week, maybe longer."

"You do realize don't you that seeing my dick, or worse, seeing me completely naked, would have turned all three of those girls into lesbians don't you?" I didn't actually believe this, but I knew he might, and Anne almost certainly would if she had bothered to think about it.

"I don't think it works that way," Lucy said.

"Anne might think so, if she ever bothered to think."

Thinking about Anne and Cinni, I recited, in my best— though admittedly not very good—Richard the Third/Hamlet mode, the following four improvised verses:

Sometimes you stand tall
Sometimes you fall
Sometimes you who know everything

Don't know anything at all.

Sometimes you see light
Sometimes it's bright
Sometimes when it's 12 o'clock you wonder
If it's noon or it's mid-night!

Sometimes I'm amazed
Sometimes just dazed
Sometimes I feel insulted when
I'm actually being praised.

Sometimes when I fall
Like a plane I stall
Need to rev the engines up
Wake up, get on the ball.

"Who's going to sing that one?" Glen asked.
"Assuming anyone would be interested in it, if I can rock it
up and think up a chorus and maybe a bridge, I'd try to shop it
with Avril Lavigne. If I can't rock it up, maybe Miley Cyrus or
even Justin Beaver. Shit, maybe even Cinni, L O L," I said,
laughing I think because I actually said L-O-L as if I was
actually Laughing On Line. "But I'm just riffing or free styling
and will probably forget it before I get around to writing it
down."
"You have every right to be mad at Cinni," Lucy said.
"She was just playing a prank on me. I'm not really mad at
her. People don't believe me when I say it, but I was actually
once her age. And I've done a lot of stupid, immature things
and I've played a lot of practical jokes that no one thought was
funny." I was very mad at Anne though, but I didn't want Glen
to know that. I had a strong belief that it was best not to let
people you were angry with know you were mad at them. Of

course, my motives varied depending on who I had resentments against and why. I usually tried to forgive people and was often successful at it.

I rarely sought revenge. Of course, if I was better at getting revenge, I wouldn't be so quick to forgive people. In Anne's case though, I'd get revenge the following night when the Mardi Gras episode aired with the "Hell is for Children" music video near the conclusion of the episode.

Lucy asked me if I wanted her to take the day off saying it was a field day—whatever that was—and wouldn't be a problem, but I told her we could have a "session" that night which I would very much look forward to.

I knew Lucy would have dumped me if I had told Cinni that she could practice blowing me, and as much as I wanted to be honest—I didn't actually—about why I didn't allow it, I couldn't tell her that first I had a moment on conscience and concern and finally I thought we might be able to make a really great episode where Cinni could go to New Orleans or even New York, and attend some kind of class to learn how to give really good face. Even if this had already been done on "Sex and the City," it would still work again with our much different demographics, the majority probably believing that the best way to give of good blowjob was to take their teeth out first.

I still thought it would make a great episode even if what Billy said was true, that she was actually good at it. My criteria for a good blow job differs greatly from the vast majority of porn I've watched and I've watched a lot. I'm sure a lot of women are good at it. But how good is good?

Two years ago, Glen mentioned that Cinni would be going to college after she finished High School. Is she still planning to? If having no money was the deciding factor that kept her from attending college last fall or this spring, it wouldn't be a factor now. She'll have enough for two years at community college just from the first season and we could probably shoot around her schedule for the second season, assuming she went to a local college.  But if she doesn't go to college, maybe she can take a few courses in cock sucking, just to learn all the different techniques.

# Chapter 22 The Mardi Gras Episode

Later that day I received a FedEx package from the *Armed American Christian Patriot* Channel with a contract to do 24 more episodes at the rate of $100,000 per episode. This was part of our original contract and we only had to sign it to agree with the number of episodes. Instead of this contract though, they also offered us an amended contract for 72 episodes spread over three seasons at the rate of $200,000 per episode, with 50% of each season paid three months in advance. They stipulated that the show would almost certainly be broadcast on their sister network, the *Glory B Good* channel, which had an emphasis on family values rather than firearms and the second amendment. Both channels were owned by a bullet and firearm accessory manufacturer named Junior Treadway.

One point they made clear in their cover letter is that they wanted the episodes to feature more of Anne Morgan-Carter, stating that they thought she added a wholesome Tammy Faye Bakker atmosphere to our show, that she should be the show's moral compass and each episode should end with her saying a prayer. They also indicated that they wanted to feature Gene as a liberal foil that Anne could spar with. Anne would, of course, always be morally and politically victorious.

Fortunately, I didn't have to let them read the cover letter.

Since Glen first told me he was going to marry Anne, I had dark forebodings that she would get her parole revoked and he'd be stuck taking care of her children. As bad as that possible scenario was, this was worse. We would, in effect, become Anne's keepers, perhaps contractually liable if she got herself in trouble. And, she would definitely want a much larger share if she knew she was now unofficially the star of the show.

Although I had been looking forward to a fuck fest that night, I decided business came first and when I went over to Lucy's place, I brought the alternative contract and the cover letter. Although she didn't currently practice law, she had a law degree and would understand contracts even though criminal law was her specialty. She shook her head when she read it saying, "Family values my ass! That cunt is as wholesome as her grandmother's asshole. And Anne is the future of the show." She shook her head again. I think if we were outside she would have spat on the ground.

"If her parole gets revoked, can she still do a half hour or so a week in prison?" I asked.

"That would depend of the warden. The odds are around 50/50, contingent on where they'd send her. Anne has done a half a dozen things that could have gotten her sent back to prison. I felt sorry for her kids and I let her slide. But I can't do that if she fails a drug test. The fact that she's remained clean as long as she has is a miracle. Can Glen keep her on the straight and narrow?"

"I hope so. But who knows. She's going to be pissed tomorrow night when she sees the episode." I then explained how I edited the "Hell is for Children" video making her look like a child abuser.

She laughed. "I don't think she would beat her kids, hit them maybe if they were doing something that could hurt them, but not actually beat them. Not the girls anyway."

She paused for a moment to think it over.

"I say sign the contract but attach a stipulation that none of you can be held responsible if she breaks her parole. I'll ask one of the lawyers who works in the DA Office if any has corporate law experience and if so, to phrase the addendum in corporate legalese, though the cable company would still have to agree with it. I've never studied corporate law above the most basic required level. It never interested me."

"It's not very ethical, but I'd just as soon not tell Anne that she is going to be the focal point of the show," I said. "She might demand a bigger share and cause enough problems to somehow mess things up. I wonder if it matters to the execs at the Glory B Good Network that she's a borderline sociopath. And why resurrect a new Tammy Faye Bakker?"

"You're not concerned about Gene?"

"Gene may take a few shortcuts, but he's not violent or stupid. He knows he's got a good thing going. I'm a lot less sure with Anne. Hopefully she'll mainly just overreact like she does on FaceBook and not in the physical world."

"That's bad enough," she said. "It doesn't make any sense the way she gets so mad at people on Facebook who disagree with her or have different political philosophies. I once counted eight swear words in one post as well as a variation of the N-Word. Maybe she'll friend a few execs at the new channel."

"They probably swear just as much as she does."

She searched for a few moments on her phone, and then started reading: "'Crazy bitchtards like Brian Ken have there heads up there ass. He thinks I'm hurt by his dumb ass deleting me well fuck ya ya fucking cock sucking retarded drama queen i dont know you anymore so no feelings hurt here and one less bitch i see posting nothing but depressing love seeking bullshit crying ass fucking stupid unreal fucking drama ass posts and ugly puppy pics every time i get on facebook geeky people and their stupid shit niggas cant handle the truth about this bitch fuck off cum chugging fuckface fag.' I can go months without saying that many swear words and if my mother saw it, I'd be embarrassed and I'm sure I would never hear the end of it."

"And her kids are all on Facebook, well, the three older ones anyway. I'm not sure if I ever heard my mother swear and although my father would sometimes say Damn and, I think, shit, I never heard him say either the F-word or the N-word for that matter, though I'm sure he said the F-word occasionally. Just not in front of his children. That's not meant to imply that Anne loves her kids any less than my parents loved me or my brothers, just that she was raised to believe it's OK to swear that way, even in front of children. I sometimes worry what might happen if she found out Billy was gay, though I doubt that he is. I sort of get the feeling she'd still love Billy if he was a murderer or a rapist or even a child molester, as long as he didn't molest boys, but she would write him out of the family completely if she found out he was gay. Hopefully I'm wrong."

"Are you sure you're a conservative?" she asked me.

"Oh sure, on most issues anyway," I said. Actually, I didn't believe in any political party. I thought it was all bullshit but that doesn't play very well down here. "But I'm also a realist." At this point, I decided to tell her my biggest political secret. "I have to admit that I'm pro-choice, not that I'm pro-abortion or anything like that. I just don't believe men," here the BS started, "have the right to tell women what to do with their bodes—not counting what they do with their bodies during consensual sex, of course."

"I getting to like it when you're on top, you friggin baby killer" she said.

"I just believe that if men could get pregnant, there would be an abortion store on every corner and they could watch sports on tv and drink beer while waiting for the procedure," which was one of the few things a liberal ever told me that I actually believed was true.

"Having said that," I added, "it's not like I believe in women's rights or any other stupid liberal causes. They should all be barefoot, pregnant, on their knees and blowing me in the kitchen. . .

"OK, maybe not pregnant. . .

"Well if you really insist, you can keep your shoes on. But come with me in the kitchen woman."

And with that, the mood was set and we were in and at it, though not in the kitchen. By this point, I really couldn't say if

I actually liked Lucy, but I liked the sex!

The next day I said that I had an important announcement that I wanted to make after they showed the third episode that night and that I wanted everyone present including Liz and Gene.   I didn't include Granny because she was usually blackout drunk by 7:30pm.

Throughout the show, there were, edited in 5 or 10 second excerpts, short previews of "Tonight's Video," coming up later, later, soon, next: two of Lindsey, one of Billy and one with both.   Otherwise, most of the show was of the Mardi Gras Parades, with some of Lindsey and Billy looking really board. We included the moral lesson with Cinni preaching against flashing to Brittney, how men don't respect women who flash and a little other BS like transvestites being on the highway to hell, etc.

Everyone liked the video, surprisingly even Anne, who seemed to be happy to be included in a music video.   I was dead wrong thinking she'd be mad about appearing to be a child abuser.

"Was that you acting Anne or Fats editing it into the video?" Lucy asked.

"A little of both.  I'm always mad at Fats and he knows it."

"I thought that you must constantly be as pissed at Fats as I am.  And the bastard isn't even videoing me."  Hopefully, she was lying here, about always being mad at me.  If not, it's something that I never noticed.

Then Lucy leaned over and whisper something to Anne. Anne looked like she wanted to laugh, but thought better of it and held it in.  Later, Lucy told me she whispered: "The sick fuck actually wanted to use his cell phone to video us having sex."

# Chapter 23  The New Contract

After the closing credits, I said: "I got what I think is good news—certainly not great, especially for Lucy and Granny, but still good. The Armed American Patriot Channel also want to air future seasons of the show on their sister channel, the Glory B Good Network at $200,000 an episode for three seasons of 24 episodes each. If we use the same share structure, that's $8000 per episode for Gene, Lucy, and Granny and $20,000 for the rest of us—over a million each after three seasons. They emphasized that they wanted more of Gene, so we might want to give him a larger share."

"I think Gene should probably get a raise," Lucy said. "but, and this is important, he not receive his payments in share dividends but as wages. Otherwise, he will have to get an additional job just as Anne also needs to be employed."

"I was wondering when I can quit my job," Anne said.

"'You have to be employed, at least 30 hours a week, while you are on parole. If you are unemployed, you have to actively seek employment. Your parole officer can and will suggest businesses that will hire ex-con's, some even without references'" Lucy said, apparently reciting part of the conditions of Anne's parole from prison. She added: "Please don't put me in a position where I have to have your parole revoked Anne. If you want to quit your job, find another position first."

"Couldn't I work for the Morgan Family Rules corporation like Gene does?"

"If you sold your shares for the duration of your parole you could be hired as an independent general contractor like Gene. You could then buy back your shares for the same rate that you sold them, usually a dollar that no one really gives or receives. You'd be paid what you receive as a share holder."

"Now that's just plain stupid. I'd want at least a few thousand per share. Probably more. Whatever they are deemed to be worth."

"You can go that route, and you'll have to pay what they are appraised at to get them back. Corporations have no conscience. If the show is successful, they could be out of your price range, maybe even you and Glen's range. Perhaps the corporation will vote to sell them to someone else. The corporation doesn't have that much money right now."

"Mom, don't be selfish," Cinni of all people said. "We would have to sell your shares to be able to be able to come up with the money to pay that much. There wouldn't be that much to pay back. Fats, how much money does the corporation have right now?"

"A little under $900 dollars. Don't forget, 92% of what we get paid goes to pay off share holders and Gene, $5,000 to various creditors and another $1,200 went to pay off Buddy, Chris and your other friends who helped with the show. At this time I suggest that Anne keep her job until at least June, assuming we take the offer and sign the contract for 3 seasons instead of just one."

"Is there any advantage to signing the contract for just one season?" Glen asked.

"We'll earn less per episode so we'll pay less in taxes. Also, we won't be contractually obligated to come up with 48 additional episodes. Those are the only advantages I see and I'm not sure the first is actually an advantage. Personally, I would rather receive four times more than only twice as much, even if I have to pay more taxes on it.

"But if Anne's parole gets revoked," I added, "we'll have to find a way to include Anne in the show while she's in prison. I'm pretty sure we can include Cinni even if she goes away to college. Including someone who's in prison might be harder. I would hope that this is a possibility, but, and I hate to put the focus on you, Lucy, but you're the expert here."

"As long as Anne stays out of trouble," Lucy said, "tests

negatively for drugs, and is employed, she'll stay out of prison. But she can't allow stupid things to happen like deliberately exposing her younger daughters to a fat man exposing his little thing to them. As funny as that may seem, and it is a funny sight, I would have to contact child welfare who would insist on either Anne's parole being revoked, or the three younger children being place in foster homes and possibly both. As a corrections officer, I can't look the other way."

"But that was Cinni's idea!" Anne exclaimed.

"And as her mother and a responsible adult, you should have told her it was a bad idea."

"Yer just mad because we were playing a trick on you boyfriend."

"And you should be glad he didn't fall for it. I'm sorry to say this, but I half expected him to," she turned to me and started saying: "Again, I'm-"

"No need to apologize again. I've accepted it and all is forgiven," not that I was ever really angry with her over the April Fools Joke. Then I added: "I'm lucky to have you as a friend, a companion and a lover." And what the fuck do you mean by "little thing!"

"Get a room already!" Billy ejaculated, and a few of them laughed, including Lucy and Anne.

"Anyway, we need to take a vote on this before I have sex with Lucy on Billy's pillow. I talked with Arthur and he'd go along with the majority. Perhaps the best way to go about this is those who want to go with the new revised contract raise your right hand. Everyone except Glen raised their right hand. Those who want to stay with the original contract raise your left hand. Billy and Glen raised their left hand. Glen, do you have a minority opinion?"

"I just think we are rushing into this without thinking it through."

"Anyone want to change their votes?" I asked.

Billy raised his hands and said, "I just think we should go with both options, or nether."

"Billy, you had one laugh tonight.   Please consider quitting while you're ahead.   If anyone wants to change their vote please text everyone before 11am tomorrow."

Of course I knew greed would win the day, but I wasn't at all sure how I could come up with 72 episodes.   Although I don't consider the ones we already made to seem like they had any quality to them, I couldn't imagine keeping our low standards up as high as we have maintained them.

"I have some other news, for this season, starting tomorrow, the $50,000 for each episode will be transferred directly to the corporation's bank account on the day following the original airing of the episode.   I should be able to issue checks tomorrow afternoon between 11:00am and 2:00pm.   Please bear in mind that the checks will be for only one episode so they will be half of what the last checks were, which were for two episodes."

By the following morning several viewers had uploaded "Hell is for Children," the one uploaded at 10:48pm the night before by MorganKrazyKristianKlanPosse already had over 50,000 views with over 3,000 thumbs up or likes and less than 100 thumbs down.   I posted links for the higher quality mp3 downloads on all the pages I could find where there were uploads of the video.   We wouldn't make much money on the songs.   Maybe a few dollars for every hundred or so downloads.   Still, anything is usually better than nothing.

Using the—now—self admitted show insider name MorganFamilyDude, I uploaded Brittney's "Paranoid" video with links to the higher quality mp3 download.   Someone must have pointed this out to the heavy metal singer Izzy Dirtnap, who had a series of Ozzy Obsbourne, Black Sabbath and even Twister Sister Tribute bands.   He even had a few hits of his own in the late eighties, but was best known for his cover of paranoid.  One of his people contacted someone at the Armed American Patriot Channel and someone there gave them my cell phone number, which was the only phone I had.

Well, the next thing you know, Izzy is on the phone and he wanted the pretty blond girl who sang "Paranoid" and "Hell's full of Children" and even the boy who was in the Hell videos to be one of the acts in his *The Absolutely Final, No If's or Butts About It, Last Izzy Dirtnap Tour And This Time We Really Mean It!* They would pay them $50,000 per show, but from which they would have to take out around $5,000 to $30,000 per show to split among their supporting musicians. She could join at any time but there were only 12 shows left on this, his last tour.  He would pay for the hotel rooms and air tickets, etc., and, he added, if it worked out, they could be included in the following year's Late Spring/Early Summer tour and maybe even later this summer if he starts having Izzypoollagas again after a few years hiatus, assuming he can find the right venues.  His one talent was finding places off season and getting as many bands as can get to play usually half hour sets over a 12 to 18 hour period.

Of course, this call lasted over an hour with no one to translate for him, and it took over 45 minutes to grasped the main points he was trying to make.  I told him I'd have to talk to her parents about it and that I'd get back in touch with him. He then told me not to try to stall for more money, that his people would never go for that.  This warning added another 15 minutes onto the phone call.  The battery on my phone wore out before I could explain that it was Lindsey's sister who did "Paranoid."

This was, of course, the dream of a lifetime for Glen, Mark and me, maybe even Lucy too.  I didn't know how Lindsey and Billy would take it.

Although I would have been able to still make it to the bank and get the checks written out, I decided to write the checks myself, once the transfer was complete. They would be a little harder to cash, but not as long as they didn't need the money today.   To avoid the same problem that we had last week, I gave Cinni and Granny their checks before I gave Anne hers, Glens and checks for the three younger kids.  It was the last day of Spring Break so Anne could take the kids to the bank to deposit their checks.

I talked to Anne about the Izzy Dirtnap offer and she seemed more positive about it, than I expected her but said that under no circumstances could Glen go.  She said that if Cinni chaperoned the kids, and if they wanted to, then they could go. As far as missing school was concerned, they could always take summer school.  Anne may have been pragmatic about her children's education, but she was very insecure about losing Glen.  She probably thought he'd hook up with some groupies, not that I could imagine any groupies who would want to hook up with him—or with me for that matter.

I talked first to Lindsey asking her if she would cover Paranoid the way Brittney did, with the lyric changes, perhaps wearing a black wig and maybe a lot of black eye shadow to get a goth look going.  She loved the idea saying she was into being a goth since she was eleven, but her mom said it was Satanic and even threatening to cut her allowance if she continued with it.   She was sure she could do a better job singing it than Brittney, but asked:

"Why isn't Brittney doing it?  It's her song."

"I think Izzy confused the two of you or forgot what Brittney looked like by the time he saw the 'Hell is for Children' video he just couldn't tell the difference.  I wanted to tell him but the battery on my phone died.  You and Billy will get the major part of 50K per show.  That's serious money."

"Not if mom decides to invest it in a Bible Camp or some other scam.  Hell, she might just buy a new car with it."

"Don't they need your signature to withdraw money from

your bank account?"

"Yeah, I'm just playing with you.  It would be funny if she invested in a Bible Camp.  Last year she threatened to send me to one.  I only got out of it by saying I'd use being away from home as an excuse to 'lose my God Flower,' as Gram Gram calls it, 'to the first booger eater willing to impregnate me.'  I even said I'd try my best to seduce one of the perv councilors into teaching me how to suck cock as good as she did."

"That must have pissed her off.  The last part anyway," I said.

"There are some things she's proud of," she said, sounding a little disgusted, "but she didn't send me to Bible Camp.  I think I could have gotten kicked out of Bible Camp.  I've read enough of the Bible to conclude that Jesus was a Liberal.  I'm sure if I told them that, that I really believed it, then they would kick me out."

"Just don't say he was gay or your mom may kick you out."

"Mom would know I was just playing with her.  She might believe I was as big of a whore as she was before she met Glen, but she would never believe I thought Jesus was gay, probably not a liberal either even if I showed her the Bible passages proving it."

At this time Billy came in from playing or something outside and said: "My Wiggaz!"

I told him what I related to Lindsey, but he wasn't anywhere near as enthusiastic as she was.  He didn't want to miss so many classes that he'd have to attend summer school.  He looked up the schedule of Izzy's tour and said that he might be able to make the first 2 shows which were on the last two days of Easter vacation and the last 3 or 4 shows.  Which made Lindsey happy because on the shows Billy wasn't on, she'd get $22,500 more.

Cinni was open to it too though she didn't want to do it for free.  Since Lindsey didn't want to pay anything for her chaperon, and Glen wouldn't be going, she would take Glen's cut for chaperoning the kids out of the musician's fee and since she was now part of the backup band, she would take another cut even though I programmed most of what she appeared to be playing onto her keyboards.  She did play a few of the keyboard parts, but not much.

Liz could only do seven shows, the first five, and the two weekend shows before the last two.

When we got this all figured out, I contacted Izzy's people and they arraigned for us to pick up airline tickets for the six of us from New Orleans to Columbus, Ohio where their next show was on Saturday night.  Our flight left Nawleans the next day at 10:58 with a 40 minute stopover in Charlotte for a connecting flight, arriving in Columbus at 3:50pm.  I arranged for Gene to pick us up at 8:30am.

And went to work on a twenty minute, all he could spare at this time, song line up, featuring:

"Paranoid"
"My Wiggaz"
"Hell is for Children"
"Hymn 43"
"Bullet with Butterfly Wings"
"Satisfaction" (Billy's hard rocking cover)

On Satisfaction, I added a fourth verse, which was a slightly reworded version of the third verse, sung from a woman's point of view, assuming she was on the rag, for Lindsey to sing, which went:

When I'm not playing with my toys
And I'm doing this and I'm playing that
And I'm trying to make some boy
Who tells me "baby you can blow me

and suck on my bag
But we won't make love
When you're on the rag"

But Cinni ruled it out saying: "No way would I ever allow her sing that, you fat bastard!"

I wasn't going to fight her on this, hoping she'd come around. But then she added: "I realize you put a lot of work into this [I didn't] so if you want I will sing it, but can I change 'suck on my bag' to 'hum job my bag?'"

"Sure," I said. "Change it however you want within the basic melody of the song." I was beginning to see a whole new side of Cinni. A side I liked even more than her looks. "Whichever words you prefer," I added.

If needed, we could add a 5 to 10 minute encore—time permitting within the strict schedule we had—using a hybrid arrangement of my favorite Rolling Stones song "Sympathy for the Devil." We wouldn't have the time to do a quick change, so Cinni, who would sing the song, would do the following introduction:

"To understand the song, please imagine Lindsey and me dressed even sluttier than we are, our big fat slob guitarist dressed like one of Justin Beaver's twink boyfriends and Billy and everyone else dressed like music industry professionals and you may understand who the real devil is that we are referring to in this song."

# Chapter 24
## Nearly Catastrophic Concert in Cleveland

Of course Gene was late.

To make things worse, Anne and Glen drove off with their only car. I had a small ford pickup that would hold, at max, two passengers in the cab, with one sitting on the center column. I had taken the camper shell off the back and would never be able to get the mother fucker on in time. I was positive I'd be pulled over if I had people in the back. This wasn't the 80's or the early 90's when you might still get away with it. At the very least, I'd get charged with reckless endangerment while those in the back would be fined for not wearing seat belts. In any case we'd be held up. I had finally decided on calling a Cab when Gene, who was 5, 10, 15, nearly 20 minutes late arrived. We quickly loaded everything into Gene's minivan, but I was sure we'd never have the time to check our instruments, but thought we might be able to carry them on the plane, all except the drums.

As we were driving away, I saw Anne driving up to the house in what looked like a brand new Mercedes Roadster and I immediately thought I had made a mistake giving her the kids money. Although she could have put $10,000 of her own money down on it, paying it off in installments over a few years, I didn't believe it. I strongly suspected she borrowed from her kid's "trust" funds to buy the car. But I truly hoped I was wrong. In any case, I was more mentally occupied thinking we would miss the plane and I was unable to get out of being in very late mode to focus on Anne's new ride.

By the time we got to the Airport, it was indeed too late to get our baggage checked, but Mark, who had some kind of Preferred Airline Passenger card, was able to get most of our instruments past security. The only thing they wouldn't allow was Lucy's base drum and stool, though she was able to take her snare drum, sticks, etc. At Charlotte, we were again able to take our instruments on the plane. I was more worried about Cinni's cheap Casio Keyboard than I was with the others because I had all of her arrangements pre-programmed on the SD Card in the back of it and I had forgotten to make a copy of it. I told her that if they didn't let her take it to remove the memory card, but I wasn't sure she knew what I was talking about.

We got to Columbus on time and a couple roadies greeted us. They drove Billy and Lindsey in a fancy limo to our Hotel to meet Izzy, etc. The rest of us, even Cinni had to ride in a van to the hotel. I asked them to stop at a music store so we could buy another bass drum and stool, but the driver said he was in the band Death's Way and that we could use their shit. He said they would be going on right before us and we could use their drum kit, or one of their bass drums if that was all we wanted, since they belonged to the band rather than their drummer, who was a complete asshole.

Later that afternoon, a half hour before we would go on, their drummer had other ideas and wanted to be compensated for lending part of 'his' kit to us. He asked:

"How about if one of the blondes blow me?"

"They're both minors. One is only thirteen."

"How about the fat brunette for one my bass drums?"

"How about it Lucy?" I asked. "BTW, did you bring your pistol with you?" I already knew she hadn't, but. . .

"Listen motherfucker," Lucy said to the Death's Way drummer, sounding angry, aggressive, assertive, dominant and like a cop all at the same time, "offering services like the use of a musical instrument in exchange for sexual favors is a class two felony in Ohio and even if you beat doing jail time, you'll still be list as a tier two sexual offender for trying to solicit sex from a minor." She paused, and changed her tone so as to appear nicer, friendly, though still a little manipulative, "As a full time officer in the criminal justice system, who's only doing this as a favor for her boyfriend, can I please borrow your bass drum for tonight's show?"

"Shit lady you can have it. And the stool also. I got an extra bass drum anyway.

"And thanks," he added. "I came in my pants when you started talking dirty to me. I don't know about your playing, but you got world class phone sex talent!" Lucy later told me that she looked at his crouch, and down one of his legs and there was a wet spot below an obvious erection, but she thought he probably pissed himself instead. I also thought he pissed his pants, probably when he thought he might end up on Megan's list. According to Death's Way's bass guitarist, who had driven us from the airport, the drummer wasn't a solid member of the group and would probably be asked to leave after this tour.

Our set went over OK. We made a few mistakes as any group might the first time they played together live. Considering we were playing in front of a crowd of around 18,000 people, we were lucky no one crapped their pants. Everyone loved Billy's "My Wiggaz," which was the only one we did totally live. Billy even added his own intro to it to mimic DMX's, saying how much he "love my Wiggaz" and had "shed blood my Wiggaz" and then asked "give me a beat wigga" at which point Lucy played the bass drum for three beats and played four 16th notes on the fourth beat on her snare drum and we all joined in on the next bar. I had written a very easy 2 measure loop for it Am CM D7 all taking two beats with and E7 for one beat on the "My" and a D7 for one beat on the "Wiggaz" while Cinni played just minor and major triads. By the end of the second verse, half the audience was chanting "My Wiggaz." It really seemed to go over big!

The audience also loved "Bullet with Butterfly Wings." It didn't get an audience reaction like "My Wiggaz" did, but they roared the loudest for our Smashing Pumpkins remake, with

"Paranoid" and "Hell of for Children" tied for third place. They didn't care for "Hymn 43" nor for "Satisfaction," though on the chorus at the end, the audience started chanting, "take your top off, take your top off" to the verse rhythm of "I can't get no, satisfaction." Cinni was wearing a black t-shirt and black jeans to match Lindsey's Black dorm shirt and black boots outfit and probably more because she was sweating like a pig than because she wanted to expose herself, she took off her shirt showing a not very revealing black bra. I thought our cover of "Satisfaction" was better than Brittney Spears' cover of the song and almost as good as Devo's cover of it.

As it turned out, Cinni's antics really got to Billy. He thought she was upstaging him. He remained cool in front of the audience and didn't say anything, but as soon as we got off the stage he starts on her. "What the fuck are you doing? You're the one who's supposed to be chaperoning us and setting an example, Cinnamon. Instead you start doing a strip tease. What if someone tells mom?"

"I was just giving the audience their money's worth!"

"They want to hear music, not to see Miley Cyrus twerking." Said the young man who didn't understand that a C Sharp was the same thing as a D Flat and was too lazy to learn more than one position of the pentatonic scale or that the major pattern was three frets below the minor pattern.

Actually, I was against it too, but only because her bra was so untantalizing. It would have been great if it was a reveling Victoria Secret bra showing a lot of cleavage.

The next day, Billy refused to do the four verse version of "Satisfaction" taking Cinni out of the singing equation. It was his last show for nearly two weeks.

We had two days off before the next show on Wednesday and I convinced Lindsey that a few of the songs she had already learned were not metallic enough for this tour. We would need two relatively short songs or one long one before we closed with "Bullet with Butterfly Wings." I suggested around twenty songs, and she settled on three, a harder rocking "Pictures of Matchstick Men" which she had heard Glen and me playing on occasion. Then she chose two other songs from the mid-60's, Cream's "Tales of Brave Ulysses" and another from the Rolling Stones, "Have You Seen Your Mother, Baby, Standing in the Shadow." These would, of course, replace "My Wiggaz" and "Hymn 43."

For the third show, Lindsey decided to let Cinni do the whole three verse version of "Satisfaction" replacing the original third verse with the edited fourth verse. She asked for it to be moved to the third song in their set, after "Paranoid" and "Hell is for Children" to give her a little rests. Instead of doing three songs after "Satisfaction," we decided to try an extended version of "Brave Ulysses" with three long guitar solos. I thought this worked out pretty good, though those who were familiar with the original probably didn't like our version, which, other than the lyrics, didn't try to mimic it's psychedelic musical features. I didn't even use a wah wah pedal on it.

We were also able to find a replacement drummer who would take over after Lucy left the following Sunday, though she was going to be able to make the Sunday Show (along with one Friday and Saturday) since our set would end around 4:50pm, giving her plenty of time to make her 7:15 flight out of Orlando.

# Chapter 25 White Trash Wiggaz

On Thursday morning, and hour before checkout, Izzy himself, wearing his red *Sicker Sistah* dress that he usually only wore onstage when doing oldies, came in the hotel room Lindsey and Cinni were sharing. The rest of us were there discussing possible songs we might do. He said something that no one understood and then said what sounded like "congratulations" and handed Lindsey a copy of *Rolling Stone*. I think they were singing "Bullet with Butterfly Wings" either Saturday or Sunday when someone took the picture of Lindsey, Billy, Cinni, Lucy and Mark. This would be the cover of the April 9th issue. It had the caption "WHITE TRASH WIGGERS" and in a smaller font "an Offensive, Crude and Disgusting Act Where Autotune Insults Autism."

"Gettin' yer picta on the cova of the Rollin' Stun is a big fuckin' deal!" Izzy said, in his incredibly bad affectation of an English accent. "Back in thir 70's Dr John e'en wrot a song about it."

Considering he was now famous, I tried to get Billy to come for the Saturday and Sunday concerts, but he said he had an important report or paper due Monday. He said he also got suckered into attending Lindsey's birthday party the on Saturday night, which was originally going to be a slumber party turning into a birthday party after midnight. Billy maintained that he'd stay up until midnight, but he wasn't going to be "slumbering" with Lindsey's "bimbo girlfriends." (Actually, most of Lindsey's friends were more like geeks and nerds than bimbos.) It's possible that he was hoping that someone would remember that it was his birthday too. . .

According to Billy, someone from the Glory B Good channel was going to set up web cams, so he was hoping the girls would behave themselves. This was something that didn't always happen at Lindsey's, Brittney's and Cinni's parties, Billy said. He added that Gram Gram was supposed to supervise things after Glen went to work.  Figuring Glen would leave for work between 10:40 and 10:45pm, I deduced that the odds were pretty good that granny would be shitfaced by then.  Of course, it didn't take Sherlock Holmes to rationalize that this could be a disaster.  So far, I never really showed the bad—mischievous really—side of the kids, other than a few innocent remarks like asking if she could flash at the Mardi Gras parade, which I assumed most people wouldn't take seriously.  Of course, liberals would find everything they said offensive, when, in actuality, they've usually behaved better than I wanted them to.  But when their behavior was bad, it was usually too bad to include on the show.

Our Friday and Saturday shows, both in my native state of New Jersey, Friday in Camden, Saturday at Holmdel, were, in my opinion, the best shows we did.  Sunday's show, also in Holmdel, was good too, but what happened Saturday night at the Morgan-Carter home would cast a dark shadow over us for the rest of the tour.

Most of this I got second hand, some third and forth hand, a lot from Lucy (as I listened to her side of her phone conversation, during and afterwards as she talked to Anne, Billy, the third "cowgirl" and one of the police officers who came on the scene after most of the evidence was destroyed and two of the major players had fled) and some from my own web cam, which I had set up to alarm me if anyone was messing around in my room.

Anyway, sometime Saturday afternoon or evening, Granny dies sitting on an easy chair with the remote control for the TV gripped in her hand.  It was apparently still in her hand as postmortem rigidity set in.  Earlier, apparently at Lindsey's request, she had stocked the refrigerator with a few—some say two, some say five or six, Glen said he saw between 12 and 20—gallons of her homemade wine.

Brittney, who discovers that Gram Gram is dead, decides

the party must go on and plays hostess to Lindsey's friends keeping everyone refreshed, though not until Glen left for work.

Around thirty minutes after Glen left for work, someone turned off the one visible camera in the room, not knowing there are several others hidden. Then two of Lindsey's friends started flashing their breasts at Billy, who was trying to watch TV and was apparently the only one there who wasn't drinking. (Actually, Billy was the only one who said he wasn't drinking.) The flashing was also apparently prearranged by Lindsey—her idea of a birthday gift for Billy.

Shortly afterwards, two other young ladies who apparently crashed the "party" and who seemed to actually know what they were doing, "seduce" Billy live, from two different angles on two web cameras. Billy theorized that one of them may have spiked his Mountain Dew with viagra or something like that. In any case, one particular part of Billy enjoyed it. To an extent anyway. After somewhere between four of five seconds and fifteen minutes of foreplay, apparently both young ladies, took turns taking the top position, and managed to satisfy themselves, leaving a somewhat nervous Billy unfulfilled.

At this point, a third, less experienced young lady decided to mimic the other two, who were apparently already gone, and climbed on top of Billy. According to several of those present, it was either her first time or her first time on top. While this is going on, the other young women at the Party who until this point, were just talking among themselves and not really watching, start clapping their hands keeping time with the young lady who, even if she didn't know what she was doing was apparently doing it good enough to eventually give Billy a happy ending. According to some reports anyway.

Some of the young ladies, according to Brittney, even ridicule and joke about the size of his Billy's penis. Billy probably left the 3$^{rd}$ young lady frustrated, but on this last point

I'm making an assumption.  Happy Birthday Billy!

Finally, a couple of the young women started taking turns french kissing him.  Whether they would have taken turns at doing more intimate things with him is unknown.

At this point the craziness ended and the insanity began when Anne got home and entered the living room, pulls the girls kissing him away from him, slapping the girl on top of him and also slapping Billy a few times, even calling him a "fag"—anonymous source—for apparently not "fucking the dumb slut like a man."

She then drags the young lady and Billy into my room, which sets my web cam going.  Here, Anne read the two the riot act about unsafe sex, and waiting until they got married, etc, and if you believe that I have a couple bridges I want to sell you.  Anne just lost any semblance to sanity and proceeds to intimidate Billy into finishing the job like a man, taking the top position and badgering him into calling her a slut, cunt, ho, bitch, skank, fuckbunny, cocksucker and so on, dehumanizing her while emasculating him.  Sometime during the coerced love making—rape by proxy—session, Anne's phone starts ringing, but she doesn't answer it.  After Billy somehow finishes—and I'm surprised he could perform at all, considering the circumstances—and is now a man in her eye, she mentions how mad she is at me for not taking him to a whore house and pulling this stunt instead.  Against all reasoning, Billy believes that I somehow set this up and starts developing all kinds of plans for revenge against me.  This last part Billy told me about around 6 months afterwards.

It was while this was going on that I got an automatic text with a link so I was able to access the web page with the video from my cell phone.  It showed everything that was happening in my room, though not the sound, through a not very high resolution stream showing Anne standing over the bed while Billy was humping someone on the bed.  I immediately called

Anne to find out what the fuck she was doing.  She didn't answer at first and I had to call her 4 or 5 more times.  She didn't answer until Billy finally finished.

When she answered I could only asked: "What the fuck are you doing?"

She tried rationalizing her madness, but I wouldn't have it.

I asked her if Billy's partner was a prostitute—actually I was hoping it was just a blowup sex doll.  When she told me it was one of Billy's or Lindsey's classmates and that she caught them doing it on the living room couch, I lost all focus on reality for a short period.

Finally, I said: "You have to make things right with the girl.  Ask her if she now understands that premarital sex is wrong and she should wait until she's married.  Read her and Billy some kind of Christian Riot Act. If that doesn't work and I can't imagine it would, offer her your next 5 checks."

"Twenty-five thousand, are you crazy?"

"Did that girl consent to what you and Billy did to her?"

"When I first found them, she was humping him like a cowboy riding a bull, putting on a sex show for all of Lindsey's friends."

"OK, try this. 'Sex should be a private thing between a man and a woman.' See if she'll buy that?"  She said it and the girl replied:

"Then why were you standing over us telling Billy to insult me?"

On my web cam I could see Billy leaned down and kissed her a few times—on her cheeks and forehead, not her mouth.  He brushed her hair a little, whispered to her and moved his ear to her mouth so he could hear what she whispered back.

"She wants $200,000 or she's going to go to the *National Enquirer*," Billy said.

"That's crazy, even Fatty suggesting $25,000 is too much," Anne said.

"Fats isn't going to go to prison, you and me are," I could hear him say to her.

Billy goes back to his whole caressing her hair act, kissing her, this time gently on the lips, before whispering back and forth to her. By this time, I was pretty sure it was Billy trying to push his moms buttons.

"Now she wants $250,000 and I have to be her boyfriend and take her to the middle school prom. She will take it in installments though. Please accept this offer before she makes me marry her."

While Billy was making this pitch—Middle School Prom, only in Mississippi—on Anne and me, Lucy got a phone call and went in the bathroom to answer it.

I tried telling Anne to tell her we'd come up with the money, but she has to give us time. She ignored me and said:

"Billy, you're both too young to get married."

"I'm sure she'll wait," he said and then turned to look at her and she nodded. By now I was sure it was some kind of shake down Billy was hatching, or maybe just a joke, though I found that kind of hard to believe, considering both kids looked like they had gone through hell just a minute or two earlier.

# Chapter 26 White Trash Wiggaz II:
## Between Purgatory and Parole

Lucy came out of the bathroom and asked, "Are you talking to Anne?"

"Ye-"

"Gimme the phone! Now!" I quickly closed the video and handed it to her.

"Anne, there are two web cams in the living room, one near the TV aimed at the couch and the other near the side door, probably on the shelf over the coat rack or hanging from it. Make sure they are unplugged. The page that was showing the feed has stopped showing it, but it's possible other sites might also be showing it. Then find out what the kids have been drinking and pour it down the sink.

"Now give the phone to Billy." Anne must have muffled the sound on her phone and told, commanded or asked Billy not to tell her what happened since she brought him into my bedroom.

When Billy finally came on the phone she asked, "Billy, what happened out there, did you initiated it? It didn't look that way but still I have to know?" She paused, listening, turned to me, gave me an angry look, shook her head, and continued listening. "We'll talk later about that. We're pretty much through anyway, but I would need more than your mom's word on something like that before I'd believe it. If the police question you, tell them exactly what you told me happened, leaving, for the time being anyway, Anne's suspicions out of it. If your mountain dew glass, OK cup, is still there let them analyze it."

At this point, she looked at her other phone, and said "Ask your friend to shout out to Anne that she get both web cams and then to dump out the booze. But I want to talk to her too." She turned on her speaker phone feature so I could her the kids shouting out a string of profanity, which I could hear even after I heard someone close my bedroom door.

"Let me talk to the girl now," she paused, she had turned the speaker off so I could only hear one side again. "OK, when she comes back. Are you OK?" she asked, and waited for Billy to reply. She then said, sounding concerned, "Billy, I'm sorry, but it's a lot worse. All of your first experience with the first girl and four or five minutes with the second girl were captured by a web cam near the TV and appeared on the Glory B Good Channel web page before someone removed the feeds from the page. Probably not that many people saw it, but there's a chance that someone did and will make copies and flood the internet with them."

"Billy says to 'tell Fats that not only does he have cum stains on his pillow, but a big piss stain on his rug.'"

She went back to talking to Billy, "You don't have to worry about that. If you only have dry orgasms you can't get a girl pregnant, or three girls... Oh, you definitely don't have to worry about that. Five inches is plenty, and you probably have a lot of growing to do. There's a good chance that *it* will grow too... Well they watch too much porn." She looked like she was trying hard now not to laugh. I just hoped she wouldn't tell him that five inches as half an inch bigger than my poor little thing. Instead, it sounded like she was trying to tell him how to satisfy a woman in bed, though without even mentioning eating pussy.

As it turn out, while Lucy was talking to Billy, Anne talked the young woman down from $250,000 to a check for $500 and permission to marry Billy and/or go to some dance with him or something. She also gave the girl a couple jugs off wine, which she apparently brought into my room to hide for the time being.

When Lucy finally got a chance to question her, she mainly wanted to assure herself that Billy hadn't initialized things with her or the two other girls and that none of them knew there were active web cams broadcasting on the web. She hung up and gave me back my phone.

"Anne told Billy the whole fuck fest, (that's what you like to call it isn't it?), was your idea. Well, was it?"

"I didn't even know there was going to be a party until Billy told me when I tried to get him to fly up for last nights show. I certainly wouldn't have condoned giving a bunch of kids wine, or whatever they were drinking."

"And what makes you think there was wine?"

"Only because Granny was involved. According to Anne, she makes homemade wine out of fruit juice, sugar, yeast and koolade."

"Did you tell Anne you would take Billy to a whorehouse?"

"No! What the fuck!" I thought about it for a few seconds and said: "I once asked Anne if I could take Billy to a sheep farm to get him, um, some sexual experience, which anyone else would have taken as a not very funny joke, but Anne asked me to stop being so cheap and take him to a real cathouse, or maybe she said whorehouse. I never had any intention of doing it. I was just joking around. Now maybe if he was sixteen or seventeen and still unlaid I might have considered it, but thirteen, or now fourteen, is too young to be messing with prostitutes."

"Hell, that's another thing I could revoke her parole for, but maybe she was joking too. Now Billy thinks you set up the whole thing. I'll ask the police to question the two girls who initiated things. I'm sure they were just being brats. Hopefully Anne won't—" Her phone rang. "Speak of the Devil. Hello," there was a twenty second pause. "Is there a police officer present? Please ask one of them to talk to me. Yes using your phone. And your minutes, which, I might remind you, are unlimited. Hello, officer, I'm Lucille Laroux, Anne Morgan-Carter's parole officer. Could you please ask the first two young women who had sex with the boy if anyone put them up to it?"

Long pause here.

"I'll have a good talk with her tomorrow morning. If we're sure the grandmother supplied the alcohol and is beyond the arms of the law there's probably no need to arrest Morgan, but if you feel you have to, have the Morgan girl stay at one of her friends houses rather than putting her through the system again. I'm sure her oldest sister would be willing to be her guardian. No, not that. She just doesn't think. You're on the scene so you can judge the situation best." She gave him her cell phone number and asked him to get back to her after he talks to the two young women.

"Young women, how old were they?" I asked, though there were a lot of things I had no idea what she was talking about.

"I just used that term in case the two girl's parents try to press charges on Billy, to make them sound more mature than Billy, which I'm sure they were, physically anyway. Sometimes someone with enough political juice can get a kid Billy's age, and even younger on a statuary rape charge, even with girls one day before their sixteenth birthday. It's rare, even in Mississippi, even when the boy is black, but it can happen."

"You think Anne knows something and is trying to somehow shift the blame on me. If anyone, I'd think Granny should be held accountable, she—"

"Gram Gram is dead. Cold even. Five or six hours at least. Anne may be trying to shield Glen, who was home when the party started. I doubt Glen had anything to do with it and the drinking might not have started until he left for work. But that won't stop Anne from making things worse." And even when she had been on the phone with the third girl, I didn't think the girl told Lucy what happened. I couldn't imagine Lucy letting that slide.

Then she added:

"If I was 100% sure Cinni, along with Glen, would accept partial guardianship of the younger kids, I would have revoked her parole when Anne went along with Cinni's silly April Fools blow job prank. I'm not 100% sure if she's an unfit mother, but she's certainly an unfit person."

"You said earlier, before all hell broke loose, that you wanted to talk to me about something?" I asked.

"That can wait. I got Lindsey's surprise party tomorrow. I got to pickup an ice cream cake that I've preordered that says "Happy 14th and Fabulous Birthday Lindsey" with 14 exclamation marks after her name. If I had known her birthday present to Billy was to get two girls to fuck the shit out of him, it would have said: "14 and Foolish. . ."

She then said she was too tired to have one or our usual fuck fests and offered to give me a hand job, at least until she fell asleep, but I pretended I was tired too, which I was— though I was almost never to tired for sex. I just didn't care for hand jobs when they didn't lead to something else. Which was true even though when I eventually jerked off before going to sleep, my final—climatic—fantasy was of Lucy giving me a hand job.

# Chapter 27 White Trash Wiggaz III: Reporters and Reprobates

Lucy was already gone when I got up around 9:30am. Since we were doing another show in Holmdel, New Jersey that night, there was no need to scramble, pack—not that I brought enough to actually unpack—check out and catch the tour bus we were assigned to. Lucy and Cinni were throwing Lindsey a surprise birthday party at 11:30 that morning. Lucy and Cinni both reminded me after the previous days set to be there and buy Lindsey something nice, and Lindsey texted me three times to remind me to be there. Waiting for me when we checked into our hotel Saturday was a Fed-ex package containing a Hermetic Cross that was platinum on one face and gold on the other and included three separate interchangeable chains, one each of silver, gold and platinum. I figured the platinum side of the cross would go well with the Black Dorm Shirt and Boots stage outfit she's been using on the tour. I had to wrap it myself, so it looked pretty bad. In the card I added that if she didn't like it she could exchange it for the silver Pentagram I got for Billy. I signed the card "from Fat Fat Fatter Fatty Fats!" Of course, a little voice in the back of my mind was saying she would probably prefer a few cans of whipped cream for their nitrous oxide content.

Lucy texted me that Anne would probably be OK. She had shift all the blame of everything that happened to her dead grandmother. I found out later that someone at the Glory B Good Channel erased all they had recorded from the point where the girls started flashing their breast—or at least they claimed they erased it all. Still they might have some video of a not very animated Gram Gram hogging the remote control. We might be able to get a few minutes of some kind of a *Weekend at Bernie's* scenario going.

I got to Lindsey's suite over an hour early in case anything needed to be done, but mainly I was hoping to get some quality time—defined blowjob in the bathroom—with Lucy. Cinni would be doing something with Lindsey and was supposed to keep her away until 11:30. I was hoping for at least a quickie, though not counting on it. Lucy was in one of her weirder moods since she got back from last night's show, an hour after me.

"Thank God you got here," Lucy said. "Could you let any early arrivals in? I have to get Lindsey's cake."

Since I wasn't counting on it, it seems, for once, that my math was correct.

"Sure, but how many people are coming?"

"Cinni invited Izzy and his people and all the Death's Way band members to thank them for lending us their bass drum. Cinni invited a few others, but didn't say who they would be. Since Lindsey is only 14, Cinni told everyone that no alcohol would be served, but I'm sure some will be bringing their own. Oh, and a reporter from *Rolling Stone* is also coming to do an interview for an article they're doing about us. Cinni said that was scheduled before the party.

"I'll be back in twenty or thirty minutes."

I didn't really know what I was supposed to do. I put coffee on. I noticed there were a couple thermal quart or liter sized Carafes in a cabinet so I washed them out and I filled them when the coffee was ready. I also noticed Lindsey or Cinni had some Chocolate Mocha coffee in a Starbucks or Seattle's Best bag, so I made some of that too, drinking most of it before the party was over, nearly half before it began. I didn't think we get very many people, but I had noticed two twelve packs of soda in a little closet or pantry in the kitchenette, so I put five cans in the freezer and the rest in the fridge, setting my watch timer for 20 minutes so those five would only be chilled rather than frozen.

The first guest to arrive was the reporter from *Rolling Stone*. He, Willie William Williams, was a freelance reporter and writer and this was only his second story that he was doing for this paper. I told him he'd have to wait around 45 minutes before Lindsey got here, and probably several more hours for an interview with her.

He asked me a number of questions, mainly about Lindsey. As a precaution, I turned on my portable recorder, but he talked so softly that it didn't really record what he was asking. Among other things, I said:

She is the best vocalist in the family and one of two who could sing and record without autotune.

No, I didn't think she had a great voice, but she had the potential to be a really good singer, considering she had never taken singing lessons and, at this stage, I didn't even think she could read music.

Yes. But she has a great ear. Better than mine and I've been playing the guitar and singing since the late eighties though I gave up singing after I quit smoking.

I don't really follow modern pop music, but I think she has a really great potential. I'd just as soon she focused on other genres of music where she would be freer to express herself. Of modern singers, Avril Lavigne seems to be the only one who is both talented and sings stuff that isn't entirely formulaic. I'd like to see Lindsey and her brother go the same root. Use their talent while singing songs that are to some extent relevant and not just about partying and hooking up at clubs.

Yes, I am old fashioned. I was raised in the 80's and 90's when there was a lot of great music out there. And my parents had a big selection of even better music from the 60's and the 70's which I came to appreciate too. Now, most of the music is crap. Pop music anyway.

At this point, I realized I was talking too much. I didn't want the article to be about me being their puppet master.

But you really have to talk to Lindsey and Billy. They will ultimately decide the direction they take with their music. I'm just their producer and lead guitarist and I'm not George Martin and they aren't the Beatles.

I've also heard rumors that something happened last night, but I haven't seen any of the web cam videos that would support those rumors.

Despite the image from our rap videos, Billy's a good kid, and, as far as I know, he was not drinking or anything like that. Nothing stronger than Mountain Dew anyway. [I didn't add that I have also heard someone say that his soda may have been spiked with Ecstasy and even Viagra.] But I don't know if these rumors have been substantiated of even investigated.

No, I'm sure the girls weren't lured there. It is more likely that they crashed the party. The most solid leads—that's what you call it, right, 'leads'?—that I've heard is that they may have been older sisters of a couple of the kids at the party. But I don't know if they were in high school or college students or just a couple of homeless crackheads. Maybe in a day or two we'll know more, but it's only been around ten or eleven hours.

Yes, he could have been here. But he was more concerned about his grades in school than these concerts which none of the Morgans were prepared for. I give both kids a lot of credit. Before last Saturday, none of them had appeared in front of a crowd larger than a school play.

# Chapter 28 Lindsey's Vanilla Birthday Party

At this point, Izzy showed up with a few friends or assistants or people he met in the hall, though I don't think any were members of his family. He asked what I think can be translated to: "Where's Lindsey, the birthday girl?"

"It's a surprise party. She'll be here in around fifteen minutes," one of his assistants said.

"I know what kind of party it is. I was asking where she is."

We had met briefly before but I guess he forgot. I told him I didn't know where her sister had taken her. He asked who I was and I told him I was her producer, music director and lead guitarist.

"Ah your the sot who thinks he can play the guitar better than Eric Clapton. Only a few people can play better than Clapton and you are not one of them."

"I never said I could play better than Clapton."

"Then don't butcher his songs."

"We were just doing our own interpretation?"

"Your interpretation sucks. But the chil' did sing it won'erfully! If you could play as nice as she sings you might have a bette' career."

At least I think that's what he was saying. It's possible he was talking about the weather. Since he was paying us, I decided not to argue with him and try to humbly accept his admonishments.

Around this time Lucy got back, arriving with a few of the members of Death's Way including everyone's favorite pervert drummer and the bassist who gave us a ride from the airport last Saturday.

"Happy birthday Lindsey!" Izzy said. He paused, then added: "But where's your sister Cinni? You didn't eat her did you?"

At this point, a couple of his assistants started laughing, as if he had just told the world's funniest joke.

I started saying that she wasn't Lindsey, but was Lucy Laroux, the drummer in Lindsey's backup band, but he cut me off saying:

"I know who she is you stupid git.   Lucy knows I'm just playing with her, right love?"

"You bet Izzy.   Has he been giving you a hard time?"   She asked one of us, though she seemed to be in on the joke.

"Just keeping me in my place."

"Izzy has one of the best senses of humor I've ever come across," she said.

"When Clapton did his own version of 'Little Wing,' did anyone tell him he wasn't Jimi Hendrix?"

"Clapton was paying homage to Hendrix, not shitting all over his bleeding songs."

Here Willie William Williams asked: "Has Lindsey written any songs?   Or Billy?"

"Nothing that they've felt comfortable enough about to show me," I replied.

"What about 'Ma Wiggers'?   Didn't Billy write that?"   Izzy asked.

"That was a collaborative effort," I said.   Actually, the only part Billy wrote was changing Uncle Fats to Uncle Fatty.

"So it was you that said all those nasty things about his lovely family."

"I admit to helping with some of the rhyming schemes.   Oh, and I wrote the verse about his new step dad, mainly about him sleeping a lot and I took liberties there when I accused him of masturbating."

"You took liberties with his 'ole family, you fuckin' wanker."

"It was meant to be taken as a humorous rap parity of DMX's 'My Niggaz,' nothing more."

"And now you going deny beating up those kids in the

'Hell's Full o' Children' video you reprobate?"

"They were wearing make up to simulate black eyes and bruises. No one got hurt."

This went on, about one thing or another until Lucy got a text and said: "They're in the elevator, everyone get ready to surprise them."

A minute or so later, Lindsey came in and everyone yelled "surprise!" Lindsey did a better job acting surprised than I expected her to. Everything went fine until she started opening her presents. She opened all of them, acting happy and giddy, saving mine and Izzy's for last. The family had fed-ex her their gifts which she opened first. One of them, we're guessing Billy, but no one ever owned up to it, sent her a dildo. She pretended—I think she was pretending—not to know what it was until Cinni whispered something to her which made her giggle for a few seconds and then start laughing for twenty or so seconds.

When she got to mine, she said, "Well it looks to small to be another dildo," which got a bigger laugh than it deserved. But she said she liked it, which was all that mattered. Then she opened Izzy's gift, which was a similar sized silver cross with a silver chain. It's card said "To ward off Demons—Izzy." This she pretended to love and hugged Izzy and thanked him for it.

But Izzy turned to me and said, "You deliberately trying to upstage me, you fat wanker?"

"How could I know you were also giving her a cross? But my card says if she doesn't like mine she can exchange it for the pentagram I got for Billy."

"Lindsey, would you please fire him. I can get you a better guitarist by tonight's show."

She didn't even pause or ask Cinni for advice, but turned to me and said: "Fats, you're fired!"

When you have a super-talented singer, you know there's at least a 90% chance they'll eventually quit the band, but for a mediocre singer like Lindsey to make such a move seemed ridiculous at this early stage in her career. But I wasn't going to make a scene. I'd pack up, go home and regroup. I still had the TV show after all.

I got to the door before everyone started laughing and Izzy said, "You really are a wanker. Can't you see we're putting one over on you?"

"Come on back Uncle Fats," Lindsey said, seeming like the first time she added the uncle in months, not that I cared that much about it. "We're just playing."

There was a part of me that nearly started tearing up. I didn't allow myself to feel to low about being kicked out of the band, but the joy I now felt was unbelievable.

Since there was no alcohol or drugs, a few started leaving. Lucy asked if I'd stay and help clean up. She said she wanted to do some shopping while she still had time before our spot at around 5:30pm, and left early too.

"Izzy actually admitted that he liked what we did with "Have you seen your mother baby..." but suggested we do some of our own stuff. I spoke out the lyrics of two of my songs, "Carriere Angst," which was about dealing with schizophrenia from the perspective of the schizophrenic and "Attention Please," which was a spoof about Bill O'Reilly's liberal war on Christmas and he said I should add them to the set. That not every song has to be a variation of some form of Heavy Metal. He said he always loved putting a few ballads, or something soft, in every set. That it adds balance and makes the heavier songs sound more edgy. At least that's what I think he said.

Everyone left by 1:30pm and I helped Lindsey and Cinni clean up, though actually, all three of us left most of the cleaning up for the hotel staff. Cinni told me that starting tomorrow, I'd be sharing the suite with them. Of course, I'd have my own bedroom. "Nothing dirty's going to happen, uncle.  So get that out of your mind.  But it'll be easier to work together."  I told them tomorrow we'd work on some new songs and asked Cinni to practice an Em-G-Em-G-C-D-G-G-C-D-G-G progression at around 132 Beats Per Minute and a Dm-Am-Gm-F-Bb-C at around 112 BPM.

All this time, the reporter "from" *Rolling Stone* was observing us.  I told him he could now interview the young ladies and left.

# Chapter 29 Cut Up and Cut Loose

I unlocked the door and entered my room and saw Lucy, laying on her back, with her head hanging down at maybe a 70 degree angle off the foot of the bed. The Death's Way bass player was kneeling in front of her upside down face thrusting a nine or ten inch cock in her mouth and maybe 3 or 4 inches, in a horizontal manner of speaking, down her throat.

"What the fuck are you doing to her?" I could see what he was doing, but couldn't imagine Lucy willingly letting someone do that to her.

"Wait your turn man," he said. "If she's willing that is."

Lucy pushed him back a little with one hand while using the other to keep him stimulated, and said: "Fats, come back in five minutes, or go in the bathroom for five minutes," she looked up at him and added: "Is that enough time?" He nodded. "One place or the other and don't interrupt until were finished." She opened her mouth again, doing her sword swallowing act.

I went into the bath room and waited. . .

I hate to admit it, but I was really starting to fall for her. At least I think I was. She was a lot smarter than most of the women I've been involved with and even if she was a little overweight, she wasn't hard on the eyes. Hell, in her own way, she was pretty. And, even more important, she was really great in bed. I was going to have to make a strong case to try to keep her from dumping me. Of course, I couldn't compete with him if she was a size queen, which I doubted. But you can never tell.

I can't say I was really shocked at catching her in the act— well maybe not that act. I noticed yesterday that she was starting to distance herself from me. But I was shocked at seeing the position she was in. Before I quit smoking and weight between 160 and 180 and didn't have 3 or 4 inches of fat around the bass of my penis, a couple women swallowed and inch or two on occasion. The ones I can remember were in the kneeling or squatting position bending my dick downward while I was standing not feeling very comfortable. I could see that the position they were in was probably more comfortable than having my dick bent downwards and it probably was for both of them. Still, Lucy never hinted she like crap like that. On the other hand, it wasn't until she wanted a favor from me that she was actually willing to go all the way, orally speaking.

Of course, I'm human and I was overcome with a number of negative emotions that were a holdover from being born in the 20th century: betrayal, anger, jealousy, love, loss, rage, obsession. All sorts of feelings I was supposed to have outgrown in college, even if I was a conservative. But a part of me recognized that I was also human—'human, all too human,' as Nietzsche would say. And a part of me wanted to behave like a school kid who fights over a girl, though I always rationalized that those fights were usually just for the girl's entertainment.

"You can come out now," the bass player said. "I'll see you tonight." I heard a door open and close. Not sure if the second statement was for her on me—though if he wanted another sword swallowing act, I would hope it was for her.

I exited the bathroom and was shocked again. Apparently the guy didn't finish in her throat or even her mouth, but all over her face. And worse, she didn't even bother wiping it off.

"I'm sorry Fats, but I guess we are through, finished, done, in case you haven't figured it out."

"I really love you Lucy. I know I never said it but I do."

"You don't even know me. You never even tried to get to know me. Shit, the only thing you ever tried to do was get me to suck your dick and fuck missionary style."

"Come on, all the times I went down on you?"

"This is 15 years into the New Millennium you idiot. Even black men from the south eat pussy now. It's no big deal anywhere except in your imagination." She paused for a minute, and then added: "And really, the first few times we did it you let me shit all over you. I really felt guilty afterwards riding your face the way I did, even though I knew you were just whoring it to get my okay to get Anne on your show."

"And what that guy just did pleases you? And why the fuck don't you wash his cum off your face?"

"Because you find it disgusting. And yes, it did please me a lot more than you going down on me, fucking me, fucking me again, and then feeling obligated to blow you. Yes, it pleased me more that your formulaic fuck fests."

"I didn't mean to dominate you like that—"

"Don't make me laugh. Dominate me? Are you serious? You're not dominate enough Fats. I like men who are going to be the man in the relationship. You were only the man because I let you."

"Hey wait a second, I'm not queer if that's—"

"I'm not saying that, you fool. Maybe it's a Type A, B, C, D, or F personality thing or an Omega Male thing! Or just a think thing, but where you think, he acts."

"Listen, I can change. I may not have a ten inch dick but—"

"There you go, blaming your inadequacy on the size of your penis. It's not what's in your pants it's what's in your head. But it's no wonder considering all the bull shit there is in there. You know, after I met you, I actually tried reading one of your books?" Then she quoted the first two paragraphs of *Polish Joke*:

"I met Ann Lip, real name Antonina Lipski, at a Sex Addicts Anonymous meeting that I went to to pick up women. Being a big fat slob who was also a horny bastard, I found Sex Addicts Anonymous the perfect place to pick up easy women—not that they were all easy. Ann was apparently thinking along the same lines though she probably really was a sex addict, or what they used to call, a nymphomaniac. Something clicked between us, and even when we weren't fucking like bunnies, we actually liked being around each other, which was weird for me because I usually didn't like being around anyone.

"When she found out I had a license to carry a concealed weapon, not an easy thing to get in New Jersey, she started using me as a backup when she needed mussel--" here she broke off, looked at me derisively, and said: "Do you know you spell muscle wrong?  Or did she need you as a backup when she needed shellfish?

"What's worse is your web page: 'Fats Beauregard, born (November 25, 1979 Forest James Beauregard) is an American writer and musician. He was—'here you should have replaced 'was' with 'is' since you're not dead yet'—known for breaking with existing literary forms, developing a new sort of semi-autobiographical novel that blended character study, social criticism, philosophical reflection, explicit language, sex, surrealist free association and mysticism.   His most characteristic work of this kind are *Polish Joke* (2002), *Mustache Rides and Mayhem* (2003), *Forensic Facials* (2006), and *Hearts, Homicide and Hermaphrodites* (2009) all of which are based on his experiences in New Jersey as a musician, body guard and bounty hunter.'

"I did a goggle search using 7 or 8 letters in it and the first thing that pops up is Henry Miller's wikipedia page.  It was copied word for word, changing only your name and the titles of your books and the dates they were published.  Other than the explicit language and the sex, you have nothing in common with Henry Miller.  OK, you use your own name in your stories too, rather than fictional names.  But that's it.  Otherwise, you're a hack and a fraud."

At this point I was pretty sure it was over, but I had to ask: "How about letting me go down on you one last time?"

"You had your chance last night when I offered you a hand job.  You could have climbed on top of me and put your dick in my face and please believed me, we wouldn't be having this conversation if you had, not *yet* anyway.  Not today anyway. But you jerked off instead.  I've made arrangements for you to stay with Cinni and Lindsey for the rest of the tour.  Please try not to molest Lindsey.  I've asked to have Anne's case removed from my jurisdiction.  In any case, I'll probably quit the department of probation and parole.  And I've sold my two shares of stock in Morgan Family Rules, Inc. to Billy.  After tonight, the Death's Way's drummer will be playing with you in addition to the set he does with his group."

And with that, she grabbed her bag and left.  Part of me actually wanted to go after her to tell her not to leave, or at least, to at wash off her face, or, at least, get a couple pictures of the new improved facialized Lucy.  But I couldn't trust myself not to upload them to a few ex-girlfriend sites and I knew it would be something that I would ultimately regret as much as I might currently relish the idea.

If I lived to be a thousand, I doubted I would ever really be able to figure out women.  I pretended I could in my teens and early twenties, but it was delusional thinking on my part. Maybe I was only delusional in thinking that Lucy was smarter than most of the women I was used to.  She certainly wasn't smart enough to see and appreciate my finer qualities, I'm sad to say.  Other than having an average size penis, I was superior to most people in just about everything.  If she had half a brain she would have seen that.

That night, the show had to go on and it did.  Repeat of the same set from the day before.  Sometime somewhere between when she left our room and got to the Arts Center, Lucy washed her face.  She apparently had to get herself all pissed at me in order to breakup with me and was now at the point where she wouldn't talk to me or even look in my direction.  I would like to say she was showing me a side that I didn't know existed, but I had to admit that I didn't try to get to know her very well.

I asked Cinni: "Did Lucy say anything to you about our breakup?"

"She's been telling everyone," she said, "that you have a really small pecker."

"Come on, seriously?" I asked, hoping she wasn't being serious.

"She just said that she met someone else and that she was never very close to you anyway."

"I talked to mom about her breaking up with you," Lindsey said, "and she said Lucy had finally gone back to eating at the 'Y' again." She gave a perplexed look and Cinni laughed.

"No," I added. "I caught her doing the nasty with the Death's Way bassist after I left the party this afternoon."

"And you didn't beat the crap out of him?" Cinni asked. "No wonder she left you."

"He wasn't raping her and law abiding adults don't ordinarily behave like middle schoolers fighting over girls on the playground."

# Chapter 30 New Songs and Insane Solutions

We had two days off before our next show in Hartford, CT on Wednesday and then another day off before we had two in a row on Friday and Saturday at Mansfield, Massachusetts.

For this show I dug up "Carriere Angst," a song Izzy suggested we do after I quoted him the lyrics.

Here again—meddling
Once again: trespassing.
You come like a thief in the night.
You say everything gonna be all right.

Is this fun—Reality?
So much fun—Insanity!
Hoping things are finally going to change. . .
Wond'ring if normal's synonymous with being strange. . .

Is this fun? Such a blast!
So much fun going nowhere fast!
I pretend i know what's going on. . .
I open up my heart and you start to yawn.

Here again: deep in debt.
Where again? I forget.
I pretend i finally see the light
That peace is just the breaks between rounds in an endless fight.

Start again, On my own.
Once again, All alone.
How could you have meant everything to me.
Why do I feel imprisoned when I'm finally free.

Is this real—Reality?

All too real—Insanity!
Knowing things are never going to change. . .
Wond'ring if normal is the state of always being deranged!

I was kind of proud of this song.  Like a typical rocker, it only had four chords Em, G, C and D, but it was in a twelve bar structure with the first four bars—Em-G-Em-G—being a mini chorus that changed its lyrics with each repetition, followed by an eight bar verse—C-D-G-G-C-D-G-G—originally ending in a double track guitar solo with one track playing mainly 8th notes while using the G Major pentatonic scale while the guitar on the second track was playing similar patterns, but mainly playing 16th notes using the G Minor pentatonic scale.  The result was not as loony as I would have liked, but still a little otherworldly.

The other song Izzy suggested had more of a ballad feel and was supposed to be both humorous and sarcastic.

Can I have your attention please!
This really needs to be addressed. . .
But first a moment of silence please
For those who have fallen in the war on Christmas.

The blood is flowing in the streets
There's so much we need to fear!
Liberals here, liberals there,
Liberals everywhere raping reindeer!

Little Billy was hoping for a present or two
From his New York Democrat Gran' mom.
He was hoping for a toy or a video game
Instead he got a holiday card letter bomb!

Oh can I have some more attention please,

There's so much we need to fear.
Santa's public enemy number one
That's why he's wearing Kevlar underwear.

Here's there's a 32 bar guitar solo followed by a transitional Key change from D Minor to E Minor, with the vocals sounding much angrier now:

It's not just bullets, bombs and knives
You're messing with our whole way of life!
The first time a child says Happy Holidays
Their Guardian Angel's condemned and sent straight to
    Hades.

Well you think you have us by the balls
As you try to tear down heaven's walls
But baby I got some news for you
The end is coming and it's coming for you!

This was followed by a 64 bar guitar solo, the first 32 bars in E Minor and the rest of the solo and song is in D Minor followed by a repetition of the first two verses.

As I expected, neither Lindsey nor Cinni understood these songs, especially the first one. Neither being a genius, I wouldn't expect then to. But the chords were easy and they gave Lindsey something original to sing. After a few hours practicing, she finally got the joke about the second song: that I was making fun on the whole premise that there actually was a war on Christmas. Not that Lindsey really knew that much about it. Just that some people said Happy Holidays instead of Merry Christmas.

I really won her over when I told her an alternate title (that I had just made up) for the song was "Distraction Seventeen" telling her something to the effect that reporters don't report real news, but rather they distracted their audience by focusing on things like Bill O'Rielly's War of Christmas and celebrity gossip and she actually bought it. If I was in an internet chat room I'd be Rolling On The Floor Laughing My Ass Off, usually abbreviated as "ROTFLMAO." It was actually from a Rock Opera I wrote about a Liberal Apocalypse based on all the Zombie Apocalypses' movies and TV Shows, only, in this case, people were turned into Liberals rather than Zombies. Much worse.

It was at this point that Lindsey started seeing me as a closet liberal like she still was. Of course, there was no way on earth that I was going to set her straight. Since Anne may have turned Billy against me, I decided I needed some allies and Lindsey and possibly Cinni were the only ones currently available. Glen would remain a friend, but he wouldn't take my side against Anne and at best I might hope is that he would remain neutral. My biggest fear was they were just going to write me off everything. The show and the music. I didn't think they could redraw the contracts at this state, but you never knew.

And with what happened at the party Saturday night, I wouldn't be at all surprised if The Armed American Patriot/Glory B Good Channels just canceled everything to do with us. Of course, they didn't see what happened in my room, which was much worse. They just thought Anne took the two kids in there to lecture them. That was the story everyone was told—even Lucy believed it. If I had not seen part of it with my own eyes, admittedly through a not very high resolution web cam which transmitted to my cell phone, I wouldn't have believed what really happened and I'm not sure I'll ever understand it. I mean the part with Anne schooling Billy on how to fuck like a real man.

What happened in the living room was believable. Kids that age do crazy things just under the influence of their hormones. Add alcohol and maybe drugs to the equation and it's easy to progress from static in the attic to anarchy in the asylum. If Billy hadn't just been on the cover of *Rolling Stone*, it might not have happened.

Enough paranoid ruminations. A few hours before the Wednesday afternoon show, I caught Lindsey offering to pay a young man working for the hotels service staff twice as much as it was worth for a half liter of bourbon, "or even vodka," and when that didn't work, she offered him a hand job in addition to paying for it. At this point I came out, congratulated the young man for passing the ethical employee spot check test. Handed him a $20 to not tell other employees they might get tested and sent him on his way.

Although I could easily see that she could have an alcohol or drug problem—I'd already diagnosed her a nitrous oxide user and potential addict—it was hard to believe that her problem was so bad that she was actually offering sexual services in exchange for any substance. That is a *bottom* most alcoholics/addicts never reach. She said she just needed something for her nervousness. That she was scared shit-less before every show and it kept getting worse.

I asked her if she wanted to cancel their spot in the tour?

"Are you crazy? Of course not! I just want to cancel my dread of going on stage."

We talked around twenty minutes about her mother's addictions, mine and Glen's alcoholism, her nitrous oxide fight with Brittney, even the booze her great-grandmother brought to her birthday party. In the end, I don't know if she conned me or I conned her, or maybe a little of both, but I made what many would consider an immoral decision to buy her a pint of bourbon a day for each remaining day of the tour and afterwards she would go to at least that many AA meetings with either me or her stepfather. It had been a few years since I had been to a meeting, in spite of my signatures Glen forged on

Anne's parole card, and I felt it couldn't hurt if I made this deal with the devil. If she was as pretty and fuckable as Cinni was, I'm sure she could have talked me into getting her quarts/liters or even half gallons/two liters, but as it was, she talked me into getting her 100 proof strengths on days she would be performing.

Earlier that day, I was thinking of all the trouble caused at 'her' slumber/birthday party Saturday, but I had forgotten it by the time I caught Lindsey doing her hand jive act. Well, I made my decision, and I would have to live with it. And there was always the chance something positive could come out of it and she wouldn't pal around with a serial killer for a few days like I did when I was the same age—well 10 and a half months older—just to get what I thought was free booze. At least I think that's why I hung around with that nut for a few days. That there were chances something even more negative than what happened to me could happen to her I preferred not to think about. Anyway, there were only four more shows after today's.

Wednesday's show went better than anyone expected. I don't know if it was the pint or half liter or whatever amount of bourbon she drank, but she put so much emotion into the War of Christmas song that I think half the audience actually believed that it was true. And she never did "Paranoid" or "Bullet with Butterfly Wings" better.

We spent several hours on Thursday traveling on one of the tour buses and then checked into our hotel. Izzy did these out of season concert tours because he got great rates at the arenas, which were mainly used during the summer for mainly outdoor events. He always booked us into the best hotels, but sometimes best meant best rates he could find for places that weren't considered to be complete dumps. On average, I say the places all had close to a three star rating.

In the case of Mansfield, MA, that amounted to a Holiday Inn and our suite consisted of three connected rooms, two doubles on either side of single with a small kitchenette. For our first night, we would all have individual rooms, though if Billy got here Friday, probably after we did our set, or Saturday, someone would have to share a room. If Billy was still pissed off at me, this could cause a problem, but Lindsey said she didn't mind sharing a room with Cinni.

# Chapter 31 Rocky Road of Relapse

Friday morning, Cinni and Lindsey woke me to let me know Billy was going to be arriving around 11:00pm and suggested I move into the middle room since Billy probably wouldn't like to be between them and me. I moved myself and my stuff to the center room, which, if nothing else, had a larger coffee pot and a much bigger refrigerator. It also had a coffee shoppe size carafe, which had stenciled on it, "Lindsey Morgan's Morning Mocha" which I immediately started drinking. I ordinarily only have four to six cups of unsweetened black coffee a day and rarely drank flavored coffee. The one exception was chocolate Mocha.

After two or three cups, I realized it was spiked with bourbon and I quickly realized I had no interest in trying to retain my nearly 16 years of sobriety, which I could have probably salvaged by going to the bathroom and puking. Instead, I went to the nearest bar and then, when one opened, a liquor store. I tried to limit myself to ten drinks, knowing I had a show that afternoon and that I would drink at least twice my limit, if not more, so after a few I tried doing the only controlled drinking I was ever any good at: Drinking just beer. Today I wasn't very good at that, but got back in time to make it to the show and even managed not to break any strings or creating a scene, etc.

I never actually stopped drinking during the show, but afterwards I really made up for lost time before blacking out. I woke up needing to piss more than I needed another drink—a good sign actually indicating I didn't wet the bed—and found my way to the bathroom. Sometime while peeing and peeing and peeing I realized someone had been sleeping in my bed when I got up. Using my best deductive skills while examining the lack of visible evidence on my face, mainly the front and bottom my chin, and throat, I deduced that I probably did not go down on a woman, at least not long enough to leave any evidence.  On the other hand, the area around my penis was a little wet and I deduced that may I may have been blown, though it could have been sweat or piss rather than saliva.  I didn't think I had sex though it was possible.

At this point, I knew I really needed a few drinks (I also needed to check my wallet, but the drink came first).

Even though there wasn't any visible evidence, I wash off my face before leaving the bathroom.  Let that be a lesson to you Lucy.

I went to the kitchenette, but couldn't find anything hard, so I took a few beers out of the fridge.  When I opened the first one, Billy's door opened and he came out, looking very serious.  He said:

"Put some pants on and come into Cinni's room.  We have to talk."  He looked at the bed, laughed lightly, in a funny-peculiar way, and said, "Lindsey's really pissed at you."

*Pin*

*Drop*

### SILENCE!

I was trying to register why she was mad without facing the obvious.

I was hoping she was mad because I drank her booze.

I was fearing something a lot more serious.

Above all, I was trying not to think; trying to, in fact, freeze my brain.

"Get your pants on."  He handed me a glass half full of gin, probably left out from last night.  I downed it in one gulp.  I found my pants and got one leg into them realizing I still had the glass in my hand.

"Any gin left?"  I asked.  "I bought two bottles this afternoon."

"In Cinni's room, a full bottle and a little over half of another bottle.  Grab your phone too."

After sitting on the bed, I got the other leg into my pants, found a pair of Mississippi slippers, also known as flip flops, picked up the glass and headed towards Cinni's door.

"Let me call her first, wake her up," Billy said.

A minute or two later Cinni opened the door. She looked really pissed, but it could have been at Billy for waking her up. It wasn't. Surprisingly, it wasn't for what I did with Lindsey, not the sex anyway—if there actually was any. . . It was at me for getting drunk. Also, for leaving the gin where Lindsey could get to it and drink nearly a quarter of a bottle.

She threatened to dump it down the sink, but let me fill up my glass a couple times. While I was working on my third glass, keeping myself between the bottles and Cinni, Billy said: "Check your phone. You have some messages from me."

There were three, each with a picture attached.

One of Lindsey on top of me in the cowgirl position.

The second showed her kneeling between my legs apparently blowing me. My "Fats" tattoo was prominent in the picture.

On the last, we appeared to be the sixty-nine position, though the only part of me that was visible was the "Fats" tattoo on my right arm.

There was a light on in the room, but my face was in a shadow and I couldn't tell if I was awake or not, or, at least, if my eyes were open. I was pretty sure they were closed. I wasn't so drunk that I didn't know I had been set up. The All American Smartphone Version of the badger game. I also knew I couldn't prove it.

Assuming I was awake, I was pretty sure I was drunk enough to have no compunction about going down on someone Lindsey's age or even screwing her, but I couldn't imagine letting her be on top though, no matter how drunk I was. Cowgirl and it's reverse are two sex positions I never like. I was also pretty sure that I was too drunk to perform sexually, even if I was able to get it up—not that the pictures indicated that I had an erection, or even a penis.

At this point, Bill said: "We could be real bastards about this, but all we want is your voting proxy for your 10 shares of stock in Morgan Family Rules, inc."

"What do you want that for?"

"Don't worry about it. You'll still be the producer and head writer. Hell, we'll even give you the creator title if you want and you can even be the announcer/narrator, when needed. But Glen is going to be the director."

He didn't say it, but I though he might add that he could control Glen better than he could control me, not that he hasn't done a good job of that tonight.

When the Morgan Family Rules corporation was set up, as far as stockholder voting was concerned, the kids would all be considered emancipated in case Anne wanted to do something really crazy and got Glen to go along with her, I thought the kids were sane enough not to want to outsource the show to India or whatever crazy idea Anne had. That the kids might have crazier ideas never occurred to me. This was entirely my idea and, quite possibly, the biggest mistake I ever made.

He added: "Cinni is going to be the musical director and she may need your help at times." Considering she couldn't read music and could only play in the keys of C, G and F Major and their respective minor keys, she would probably need a lot of help.

"And you I suppose," I asked, "want to be the star of the show?"

"No! You're dead wrong there wigga," he said, and I perceived a very angry inflection in his pronunciation of "wigga."

"Me and Lindsey want off the show except to launch music videos—videos that we will produce ourselves! But that's it."

"So you and Lindsey are in this together?"

"We have different reasons for wanting to be off the show.

But we would both rather be singers than acting on *this* show."

"And that's why you want off the show?"

"You can ask her what her reason is when she sobers up. Mine is because of the white trash themes of the show. I don't want nothing to do with it and want to stay as far away from it as I can. Laroux, who can be more white trash than mom and Glen when she wants to, was so disgusted by the white trash character of the show that she sold me her shares for two dollars even though they were possibly worth thousands. I'm sorry she dumped you, by the way. I thought you made a great couple."

"And you're going to take the white trash elements out of the show?"

"No, we're just going to remove us from it. We'll have a video or two to present with each show or episode, but that's it. Maybe our names will appear as associate producers. Maybe. And we have a few ideas to make it even more white trash if mom, Brittney, Glen and Gene want to go that way."

"And is that what you want Cinni?" I asked.

"I don't want to have to be Lindsey's keeper. All I had to do was keep her from drugs and drinking and thanks to you I failed. If mom finds out about this she'll kill me." At this point she looked at Billy as if he might tell mom. He said:

"As long as Fats signs over his voting proxy, no one has to know. If not, well it was his booze that she drank, so mom will be much angrier at him. And maybe him going to prison will alleviate the situation. I have a contract for you to relinquish your voting proxy while retaining your royalties. It's simple and straight forward."

They both looked at me.

"How long is the contract for?"

"Fifteen years, not that the show will last that long. And you keep your share of the money—20% gross, approximately, after we start deducting corporate taxes. It's just your voting proxy I'm—we're—interested in."

He really thought this through.  Apparently 15 years was the statute of limitations for sex crimes in Massachusetts.

"You could try for a diminished capacity defense and maybe get off with house arrest—not our house, of course.  But then you'd be on the list of registered sex offenders and Lindsey would probably be able to sue you for all your holdings in Morgan Family Rules inc., and the same thing would be accomplished."

"Can I get a lawyer to look at the contact?"

"Of course, but it's fairly straight forward with no fine print."

And they had me, hook, line, sinker—Fatty Gumbo.

# Chapter 32
# Full Fathom Five Thy Bull Shit Thrives

I got through the next three shows without committing any major crimes that I was aware of and then signed myself into rehab. I was certain it was going to be harder to get and stay sober this time and that I might actually have to work some kind of program. Do more that just say The Serenity Prayer and go to a few meetings. While I was in rehab, I received a contract to sign on as producer and announcer as well as the main writer for Morgan Family Rules. I wasn't sure why they needed an announcer, but I ended up signing it without giving it much thought.

After I got out of rehab, I went to the Morgan-Carter home to pick up my junk. They offered to rent me Granny's trailer, which I ended up buying and moving to a trailer park on the other side of town. This was only temporary. I would later move back to Picayune, to the same apartment complex I was in before, though in a different unit.

Lindsey told me that I had been zonked out when Billy took those pictures and that Cinni wasn't really in on it—the setup anyway. Lindsey added that the only reason she did it was to get back at me for drinking all her bourbon laced Mocha. Maybe some day she'll understand the irony in that. In any case, considering I both blacked out and passed out, I was glad nothing happened—or, at least, that I didn't do anything to her. She also said she *probably* wouldn't have gone along with Billy to the point of going to the police. Lindsey, who had also just gotten out of Rehab, told me all this was an attempt to make amends to me and she did seem genuinely sorry. Anne told me Lindsey didn't actually have a drinking problem, she just partied too much and did crazy things when she was drunk. Anne also said she thought going to rehab would be good publicity.

Lindsey may have thought her mom was in denial, but

didn't say anything to her face.  When Anne left us alone for a minute, she also told me her reason for wanting to be out of the show was political.   That she hated her family propagating what she called "right wing propaganda" and wanted no further part in it.  She didn't care about the white trash stuff, just the politics.  Considering that she was only fourteen, I figured it might not be for 10 or more years before she realized the idiocy of liberal politics, but I wasn't crazy enough to try to set her straight.  With a little luck, maybe Anne might someday have a stroke arguing with her about it.

When she got out of rehab, she said she'd only come home it she could get my room, which both Billy and Cinni were fighting over.  Anne gave in to Lindsey on the condition that she not get caught drinking again until she was at least sixteen and could probably handle it by then.  I moved everything from the room except **the American Patriot God and Gun Safe model 24H, which was designed to keep Guns safe and in a special humidity controlled cabinet on the upper shelf to keep ammunition and even the Holy Bible dry.  I'm sure this safe will bring it's new owner years of joy and that they too will gladly endorse this fine product.**  I had bolted it to the wall and didn't feel like unbolting it, so I gave it to Lindsey along with both sets of keys to protect her valuables.

Anne had wanted to get breast implants, but someone at the Glory B Good channel said that would be a deal breaker, but after next season they would rethink it and she seemed satisfied with that.  They did suggest that she should wear more eye makeup to get a Tammy Bakker look going and eventually developed her own Sister Anne Morgan Brand of Eye Shadow, which they would finance.

Glen still slept a lot, but conceded he might quit his job at Walmart if he thought the TV thing might actually work out.

It was also while I was in rehab that Billy peeked at No. 2 in the top 40 Pop charts with "B Street Billy," something I had written more than half of for him and given him my complete rights to. More surprisingly, it peeked at No. 1 on Rap charts, though most Rap fans who bought it only got it because they thought it was a joke, which, of course, it was. Billy also charted with "Sinful Girl," which he turned into an electronic pop music mess, unrecognizable from its Christian Rock origins. He decided to get serious about being a musician and singer and started taking guitar, keyboard and vocal lessons. He also enrolled in the Berklee School of Music's Online Campus and would eventually enroll in a bunch of courses covering everything from Music Theory, Song Composition to Production and Engineering as well as advanced courses in Guitar and Keyboards. Pretty good for someone just entering his freshman year in high school.

As far as I could tell, there were no videos floating around the internet of his wild birthday sex romp. Just vague rumors that weren't believed. Considering there were eight or ten witnesses, the idea of it being kept a secret is unbelievable. Even the Rolling Stone writer, who must have known something, never followed up on it. Not yet anyway.

But Billy's real genius was actually in combining television formats creating a white trash "dog pound" experience. He successfully pitched the idea that Morgan Family Rules!!! should move from the reality TV Show genre to a more stable talk show format combining The PTL Club (later called The Jim and Tammy Show), the satiric Night Stand with Dick Dietrick, and both The Morton Downey, Jr. Show and The Jerry Springer Show, while incorporating Crowd Funding and silly videos, mainly music. Sister Anne and Brother Gene would sit on a stage in front of the most white trash audience they could find. Cinni sat at her keyboard to the right of the stage with three male identical triplets backing her up on Guitar, Bass and Drums. As a running gag, Cinni was dating one of them, but couldn't remember which one.

Brittney would make appearances either on video or on the chair or couch to the left of Anne's and Gene's desk with tabloid television news reports.  Brittney would also introduce the subjects in the audience usually undergoing hardships in the Crowd Funding section of the show where they would use the medium to raise funds for operations, wheel chairs, dental work, still repair and even bail money.  Brittney proudly stated that we only took 1% of the proceeds unlike some other crowd funding venues, without mentioning that we also took another 50% to cover additional expenses.

Aside from the crowd funding scam—actually a pretty good idea but, immoral because of the exorbitant profiting on people's hardships—I thought Billy's new format would have been brilliant.  The problem was that everything was taken seriously.  The part of the show that I hated was my new position as the announcer.  It turned out that the announcer was also the sidekick of Sister Anne and Brother Gene in the fashion that Ed McMahon from the old Tonight Show or *Hey Now* Hank Kingsley from the Larry Sanders Show was a sidekick.  And, of course, I would also sit on the chair or couch to the left of Anne, from the viewpoint of the audience with guests sandwiched between us.

\* \* \*

During our first show, our main guest was the author of the book *Why Liberals Hate God Even More Than They Hate America*.  Near the end of that segment, Anne would go out into the audience with a cordless microphone and let paid stooges ask prepared questions. But first, to add a final touch to the first segment, while wrongly paraphrasing the New Testament, Anne said: "It would be easier to drive my Mercedes-Benz through my wedding ring, than it would be for a liberal to get into heaven."  And although I had written—or re-written actually—the phrase, there was a part of me that was sickened by it in an existential nausea sense.

The *Amen_S* prompt sounded in my earpiece and I said, "Amen Sister!" hopefully showing more animation than the machination I felt like I had now become. Shortly afterwards, someone sent the que to Cinni to start singing the old Janis Joplin song "Mercedes Benz" which she sang, sans autotune, while Anne walked from her desk to the audience.

While Cinni was superficially singing I was thinking about the prospect of getting ass raped in prison and wondering if it would be that much worse than being here.

# Afterword or it Sucks Being a Sidekick

I realize my character might be perceived as, in some ways, despicable—that it might be inferred that I was an agent of chaos rather than, ultimately, a victim of circumstance and some very manipulative people living on the fringes on civilization. Having said that, I will always be a little pissed at myself that I could never get Billy to dress in Hot Pants and a tight Crop Top shirt. Capturing Anne's reaction would have been TV magic! That my Moriarty was this wimpy 14 year old just finishing middle school is quite embarrassing and hard to admit. But I have to admit that, like in the classic Greek Tragedies, it was a fault—or perhaps even several faults—in my character that brought about my downfall.

I had thought about rewriting this in the third person and using a pseudonym, but I wanted to be as thorough and honest as possible while telling this simple story. As I stated at the beginning of this book, I never lie. This is my testimony to the truth. Ultimately, I can't blame myself for any of my actions which might be considered immoral or unethical. I blame our modern media centered superstar worshiping society for developing a culture which places profit before product and where the ends always justify the means.

Proving that God has a sense of humor—not that I'm sure I believe in God after all the trials and tribulations I've been subjected to recently (someday I may even relate how Brittney beat the shit out of me just for suggesting that she "should consider losing a little weight")—I've won the Republican primary for Mississippi's 5th Congressional District. Although I plan on doing everything I can to lose the general election, including things like already getting caught—and photographed—going down on my democratic opponent. Still, I wouldn't be surprised if I win the general election. I won't get into my reasons here, but the last thing I want to do is be involved in politics.

# Wait Wait Wait Wait Wait Wait Wait!

I didn't go down on a man. My democratic opponent is a woman. Kind of attractive actually, though much too liberal to actually like as a sexual being you might sometime have to talk to.

# About the Author

Fats Beauregard, possibly a nom de plume, and definitely a character, is an adult graduate of Raritan Valley Community College in North Branch, New Jersey. In addition to writing and being a musician, he has worked as a farm hand, an actor, a warehouse & scrapyard laborer, in hotel/motel maintenance, at a car wash, in construction as a carpenter and mason's assistant, as a plumber's assistant, in landscaping, as a clerk, a computer programmer, a computer consultant, a web developer, and finally as a tutor in philosophy, psychology, computer fundamentals and applications, and in BASIC, Pascal and microcomputer assembly language programming. He has repeatedly denied being a grifter. He is currently working on his master's degree at the University of Karmic Comedy with no plan of graduating in this lifetime.

After *A Whiter Shade of Trash*, he plans to release a Political Tragedy, or perhaps Travesty, currently titled *The Prostitution of the United States*. This will be followed by the third book of the Trilogy, if he can stay out of prison.

Email Address: fatsbeauregard@gmail.com

Web Page: http://fatsbeauregard.info

FaceBook Username: http://facebook.com/fats.beauregard

40727049R00135

Made in the USA
Middletown, DE
21 February 2017